GAS TURBINE
MANUAL

In memory of I. E. ROWE
United Gas Corporation
for his inspiration

GAS TURBINE MANUAL

Prime Mover and Large Tonnage
Air Conditioning Sales & Promotion Committee
American Gas Association, Inc.

THE INDUSTRIAL PRESS, New York, N.Y. 10013

GAS TURBINE MANUAL

Library of Congress Catalog Card Number: 65–13380

Contents

v

CONTRIBUTING COMMITTEE

Introduction. W. F. WRIGHT, Director of Utilization, Southern Union Gas Company, Dallas, Texas.

Chapter 1. GAS TURBINE COMPONENTS AND CYCLES
P. B. GARNER, Project Engineer, Industrial Gas Turbines, AiResearch Manufacturing Company, Phoenix, Arizona.

Chapter 2. GAS TURBINE ACCESSORIES
JAMES R. PHILLIPS, Manager, Commercial Turbine Sales, Solar, a Division of International Harvester Company, San Diego, California.

Chapter 3. FUELS
R. L. BEARDSLEY, Industrial & Commercial Sales Manager, Washington Natural Gas Company, Seattle, Washington.

Chapter 4. SYSTEM COMPONENTS
LEONARD O. MJOLSNES, Project Engineer, and LLOYD E. HULL, Designer, The Boeing Company, Seattle, Washington.

Chapter 5. INSTALLATION REQUIREMENTS
ERIC A. WYETH, Application Engineer, Orenda Industrial, a Division of Hawker Siddeley Canada, Ltd., Toronto, Ontario, Canada.

Chapter 6. APPLICATIONS
ROBERT P. ATKINSON, Preliminary Design Engineer, Allison Division, General Motors Corporation, Indianapolis, Indiana, and A. H. WILLIAMS, Director of Marketing, Energy Systems, Thompson Ramo Wooldridge, Inc., Cleveland, Ohio.

Chapter 7. MAINTENANCE AND OVERHAUL
ROBERT P. ATKINSON, Preliminary Design Engineer, Allison Division, General Motors Corporation, Indianapolis, Indiana.

Chapter 8. ESTIMATING GAS TURBINE PROFITABILITY
W. F. WRIGHT, Director of Utilization, Southern Union Gas Company, Dallas, Texas.

Introduction

This manual has been prepared by the American Gas Association to provide information of a general nature to plant design engineers and others engaged in the application of turbines to the industrial and commercial market. As a prime mover, the gas turbine possesses most of the qualities of other engines, and many advantages of its own. Direct firing, low ratio of weight to horsepower, lack of vibration, and power output in the form of rotative motion are distinct advantages not enjoyed by any other direct fueled engine presently available.

Although the gas turbine in itself is competitive in first cost and operating cost with the highly respected steam turbine and its auxiliaries, it is possible to improve upon gas turbine performance characteristics by the addition of heat recovery devices. One of the primary aims of this manual is to make design engineers aware of the potential of the gas turbine as a part of a total energy system.

To achieve this end, the chapters following will deal with the various means by which the basic simple cycle turbine may be integrated with other devices to achieve an efficient power plant cycle. Such a plant normally will provide the operator with all of the forms of energy necessary for production purposes. Therefore, it is evident that a searching examination of plant energy requirements will be helpful in establishing desirable performance characteristics of a plant. A survey of this type should, by all means, cover the current plant consumption of various forms of energy. However, the survey may uncover many uses for surplus energy which can improve production processes or environmental conditions. Such unexpected improvements in production or environment oftentimes will justify the original expenditure regardless of other considerations.

The complete energy system concept is not a new one, but it has not been widespread in its use in recent years. Basically, it involves the development of the entire heat, light and power requirements of a plant or building complex through on-site generation and maximum utilization of any available waste heat for plant heating and process needs. The failure of American commercial and industrial enterprises to adopt this concept has been based upon the success of the electric utility industry in promoting an image of dependability and convenience for purchased power. While purchased power admittedly is subject to very few major interruptions, this does not necessarily mean that the same is not true of on-site generation. In addition, the relative convenience of purchased power diminishes in relation to the increase in the customer's usage of power. Dependability of utility service provides a financial motive for its use or purchase. Convenience of a utility service provides an intangible or emotional motive for its use or purchase. When the cold economic facts are examined, the emotional value of convenience of use generally will be overbalanced by the economy of a complete energy system.

With the vast expenditures required for industrial research and the growing threat of foreign competition for world markets, American industry no longer can afford to overlook the economic advantages presented by the total energy system concept. As industrial and commercial firms begin to place greater reliance on computers and other programmed control devices, the total usage of mechanical-electrical energy will be increased while the usage of human muscle power is diminished. As a result, the cost and dependability of the various forms of energy utilized in industrial settings will become increasingly important. It is inevitable that the cost of such energy will exceed that of manpower in the computer controlled automatic production line of the future.

This changing pattern of energy usage, while making the energy system concept appear to be quite profitable for the owner, will demand a high order of dependability for the delivery of energy to the point of consumption. Many industrial and commercial turbine installations have reliability ratios in excess of 99%. This excellent performance record for gas turbines arises from the simplicity of the basic turbine cycle. The absence of high operating pressures, absence of unbalanced forces found in reciprocating engines, and the low weight-per-horsepower combine to make it an ideal supplier of shaft power and hot gases. As a producer of shaft power, the turbine may be utilized for power generation, pump or compressor drive, and many other applications requiring a dependable shaft power output. Availability of exhaust heat from the turbine is a bonus quality which makes it possible to develop a powerhouse package superior to any other in the thermal power market. When its initial cost is compared to that of the more complicated steam turbine cycle, the gas turbine plant requires lower initial investment. It is in the fields of energy savings and lower manpower costs that the gas turbine excels. With normal heat recovery from the exhaust stream and the production of shaft power output, it is possible to recapture 75% to 80% of the total fuel input to the turbine throttle. Although modern boilers in steam power plants may be operated at efficiencies approaching 90%, the overall station efficiency falls below 40%. This drop in station efficiency is caused by turbine-generator losses, condenser losses, and the consumption of power by pumps, cooling towers and other plant auxiliary equipment. When the gas turbine is used in "dry" cycles, practically none of the plant output is consumed by auxiliaries. In other installations, a minor portion of the plant output may be consumed by auxiliaries such as boiler feed pumps serving an exhaust heat boiler. The low manpower requirements of a gas turbine plant may best be illustrated by the fact that many turbines currently in use are operated on an unsupervised basis, having the control function performed from a remote location.

Although history records a few heat-operated turbine wheels, the first commercial gas turbine was produced by Brown Boveri in 1921. In succeeding years, little progress was evident in this field until 1938, when the first pure jet military aircraft was flight tested. Earlier development of this superior aircraft by Germany might well have turned the tide in World War II had the military jet-powered airplane been available during the early years of that conflict. Because of its tremendous military significance, major industrial nations have concentrated on the development of the jet aircraft turbine in the years following the war. As a result of this concentration of effort on military jet aircraft, the jet type aircraft has revolutionized commercial air transportation and is beginning to invade the fields of private and corporate air transportation. Aside from the obvious advantage of greater speed than that of the piston engine aircraft, the pure jet has posted a remarkable record of dependability in commercial aviation. Statistics from the Federal Aviation Agency indicate that in the first ten months of commercial jet aircraft service, the jet type engine was proved to be twenty times more reliable than the conventional piston engine.

It is interesting to note that the total worldwide installed horsepower in the mid-1960 listing compiled by *Gas Turbine Magazine* of total industrial and commercial turbine installations was approximately 5,800,000* for all units over 1000 horsepower. A year later, the total horsepower installed was about 7,000,000—an increase of approximately 20% in a period of one year. By July, 1964, equipment having slightly over 9,200,000 horsepower had been installed, bringing the total horsepower to over 16,200,000.

As of mid-1962, fifty-one different gas turbine manufacturers had provided specification data to *Gas Turbine Magazine,* covering 319 models ranging up to 53,000 hp. Two years later, as of mid-1964, this had grown to eighty-four manufacturers providing specification data, to the same magazine, on 538 gas turbine models.

The profitable application of a gas turbine to a specific market is dependent upon the general economic factors governing the market and upon the local influences of manpower, fuel and electric energy costs.

Electric power generation is one of the fields where the gas turbine has gained rapid acceptance. Many of the power generation gas turbines installed by electric utilities provide peaking power at locations remote from the base load station. The smaller space requirement, low noise level, and dependability of operation on an unattended basis make this prime mover quite attractive for peaking service. In such cases, the high efficiency attained by the use of heat recovery apparatus does not warrant expenditures for such equipment because of the extremely low load factor of a peaking station. In nearly all cases, the simple cycle turbine is chosen for this service because of its lower installed cost. In other electric power generation installations of a base load character, it is accepted practice to use a recuperative type of turbine or to use some other type of heat recovery device. In some cases, a gas turbine is used in a combination cycle with steam turbines. The hot gas turbine exhaust stream, which is rich in oxygen, provides preheated combustion air for the boilers generating steam for the turbines. In this manner, the heat rate of the generating plant can be reduced substantially without incurring the costs of high temperature-high pressure equipment required for an equivalent improvement in plant heat rate.

---

* Adjusted to include units of 1000 to 1800 hp.

Process heat and steam requirements of industry often may be met through the use of a gas turbine energy package. Simultaneously providing by-product plant heat and shaft or electric power, this prime mover offers savings and flexibility of operation not available with any other system, particularly in comparison with the outright purchase of fuel and electricity under demand-commodity rates.

Following World War II, the demand for air conditioned office and retail sales space has caused a complete renovation of many commercial buildings in metropolitan centers throughout the country. The addition of the air conditioning energy load to normal lighting and power loads has increased power consumption in many cases by 100% and has required a complete overhaul of the existing building wiring system. In commercial office buildings, shopping centers and other rental space, the need for flexibility in utility services poses one of the greatest problems to the landlord. For this reason, central heating and air conditioning systems have become the rule rather than the exception in buildings of high quality construction. When the decision to install a central system has been reached, it is natural to consider the means by which it may be operated most economically for the service desired. The energy system concept offers the landlord a dependable source of heating, cooling and electric power which in turn may be sold to tenants at considerable profit. In addition to such commercial applications, process industries, such as the chemical, petro-chemical, steel, cement, and paper, and other power consuming plants, constitute a market for the energy system concept because the utility costs for such plants represent one of the greatest single items of expense. *Power* magazine (April, 1962) reports that the worldwide plant energy purchases for Standard Oil Company of New Jersey in 1960 amounted to $105.5 million, or more than the total cost of all materials and supplies for the 45 refineries involved. In this case, a reduction of utility costs of 10% to 15% would bring about substantial dollar savings.

At present, each installation of a gas turbine energy package must be tailored carefully to meet the requirements of the customer because no standard packages are available. Current interest in the standard package concept, as well as increasing sales by gas turbine manufacturers, indicates a strong trend toward the development of energy system packages. With increasing sales and greater depth of experience in the industrial market, manufacturers currently predict 10,000 to 20,000 hours operation for gas turbines prior to major overhaul. With increased line production and a change from job shop operations, it is inevitable that the moderate cost of gas turbines will be reduced considerably. As almost all manufacturers currently produce on an as-ordered basis, today's gas turbine is a custom-crafted machine with an identity of its own. It has been predicted by some manufacturers that the gas turbine can be produced for $20 to $30 per "real" horsepower when the demand warrants tooling up for sufficient volume. Engineering development programs have proved the feasibility of gas turbines capable of operating throughout the 40% to 100% power range at less than 0.45 lb. fuel per hp-hr. At this level of fuel consumption, the gas turbine can compete economically with the highly efficient diesel or gas reciprocating engine. The Army and Navy have sponsored a program for the development of a 600 hp turbine having a brake specific fuel consumption of 0.4 lb per hp-hr. At the same time, some manufacturers are developing dual fuel firing for gas turbines to permit the operators to change fuels under load. As most gas utilities have "interruptible service" rates, it is advantageous to the owner to use this clean burning fuel during the utilities' off-peak load period. However, a need exists for combustion equipment which may be switched automatically from natural gas to liquid fuel during periods of gas curtailment or service interruption. As with other products, demand for such equipment undoubtedly will produce an adequate supply.

Basically, the gas turbine industry in the United States has evolved from a few firms producing prototype military jet turbines in 1946 to several dozen large industrial firms producing thousands of jet engines every year. The aircraft market is approaching saturation, and it is only a question of time before the automotive market is penetrated by the gas turbine.

The availability of a wide variety of gas turbine engines now in production or in advanced stages of development, coupled with the increasing reliability of the gas turbine due to extensive experience being accumulated, all point to a bright future for the gas turbine.

Glossary of Terms

Gas Turbine: A gas turbine is a rotary prime mover in which a gaseous working medium, usually air, is compressed, heated and expanded to produce useful power.

Multiple-Shaft Gas Turbine: A multiple-shaft gas turbine is one in which the rotors of the mechanical components are arranged on more than one rotating shaft. These shafts may or may not rotate with a fixed speed relationship. When no fixed speed relationship exists between shafts, all except the output power coupling shaft are known as floating shafts.

Gas Producer (Gasifier): A gas turbine having one or more shafts which produces hot discharge gases and no mechanical output power.

Power Turbine: A power turbine is a mechanical component in which a portion of the thermal energy of the working medium is converted to mechanical energy and utilized to drive the connected load.

Single-Shaft Gas Turbine: A single-shaft arrangement is one in which the rotating components are mechanically coupled together on a common shaft.

Two-Shaft Gas Turbine: A gas turbine having a gasifier (gas producer), consisting of a compressor, combustor and turbine, on a common shaft, and a power turbine (fixed turbine) on a second independent shaft. Another type of two-shaft machine is the *two-spool gas turbine* which has the compressor split in two parts. The high pressure portion of the compressor is part of the gasifier (high-pressure spool) while the low pressure compressor is on a common shaft with the power turbine. Thus, the power turbine shaft (low-pressure spool) is concentric with, and extends through, the hollow gasifier shaft.

Air Bleed Turbine: A gas turbine having a capability of supplying compressed air which is bled from the engine compressor.

Open Cycle: An open cycle is one in which the working medium enters the gas turbine from the atmosphere and discharges to the atmosphere.

Simple Cycle: A simple cycle is a cycle in which the working medium passes successively through the compressor(s), combustor and turbine(s).

Compressor: A compressor is the mechanical component in which the pressure of the working medium is increased.

Axial Flow Compressor: A compressor in which the flow takes place in an axial direction essentially parallel to the compressor shaft.

Centrifugal Compressor: A compressor in which centrifugal force causes radial flow outward from the compressor shaft.

Combustor: A combustor is that mechanical component of the combustion system in which fuel is burned to increase the temperature of the working medium.

Turbine: A turbine is a mechanical component in which the energy of a working medium is converted to mechanical energy by kinetic action on a rotary element.

Axial Turbine: A turbine in which the flow takes place in an axial direction essentially parallel to the turbine shaft.

Radial Turbine: A turbine in which the flow is essentially radially inward toward the turbine shaft.

Exhaust Heat Recovery: The process of extracting heat from the working medium leaving the gas turbine and transferring it to a second fluid stream.

Exhaust Heat Recovery Cycle: A cycle in which the working medium passes successively through the compressor, a regenerator (or recuperator), combustor, turbine(s) and regenerator (or recuperator).

Recuperator: A recuperator recovers and transfers heat from the working medium leaving the gas turbine to the working medium entering the combustors.

Regenerator: A regenerator recovers heat from the working medium leaving the gas turbine and transfers it to the working medium entering the combustors by means of a mechanical device, which is usually a slowly rotating drum heated by the exhaust gas at one position and dissipating its heat ahead of the combustor after rotating to another position.

Effectiveness: The percent of available heat that is recovered in a regenerator or recuperator.

$$\text{Effectiveness} = \frac{(\text{Burner Inlet Temp.}) - (\text{Compressor Exit Temp.})}{(\text{Exhaust Temp.}) - (\text{Compressor Exit Temp.})}$$

Reheater: A combustor usually located between the gas producer turbine and the power turbine to increase the temperature of the working fluid and power output of the power turbine.

Intercooler: A heat exchanger located between two compressors to reduce the air temperature entering the high pressure compressor and thereby reduce the power to drive it.

Heat Consumption: The quantity of heat used per unit of time under specified conditions. It is expressed in Btu per hour based on the higher heating value of the fuel.

Heat Rate: Heat rate is the unit heat consumption of the gas turbine. It is expressed in Btu per horsepower-hour or Btu per kilowatt-hour based on the higher heating value of the fuel.

Specific Fuel Consumption: Specific fuel consumption is the quantity of a stated fuel used per unit of work under specified conditions. It is expressed in pounds per horsepower-hour or pounds per kilowatt-hour for liquid fuel operation or in standard cubic feet (scf) per horse-power-hour or per kilowatt-hour for gaseous fuel operation. (For fuel consumption in terms of Btu per unit output normally recommended see *Heat Rate*.)

Plant Thermal Efficiency: The ratio of the energy delivered by the turbine power plant to the heat supplied by a particular fuel. It is expressed in percent based on the higher heating value of the fuel.

Rated Power:

a. *Normal Rated Power* is the stated power of the gas turbine when it is operated under the conditions of 80 deg. F and 14.17 psia at the inlet; and discharges to 14.17 psia.

b. *Site Rated Power* is the stated power of the gas turbine when it is operated under specified conditions of compressor inlet temperatures, compressor inlet pressure, and gas turbine exhaust pressure. It is measured at or is referred to the output shaft of the gas turbine or to the generator terminals.

Rated Speed: Rated speed is the speed of a designated shaft(s) at which rated power is developed.

Normal Operating Conditions: The following shall be considered normal operating (NEMA) conditions for the determination of ratings and performance. The inlet conditions shall be measured at the engine inlet flange, and the exhaust condition shall be measured at the engine exhaust flange with simple cycle operation and at the regenerator exhaust flange with regenerative cycle operations:

Inlet Temperature—80 deg F
Inlet Pressure—14.17 psia = 28.86 inches Hg. abs
(Standard pressure for
1000-foot altitude)
Exhaust Pressure—14.17 psia

Direction of Rotation: The direction of rotation of a gas turbine is the clockwise or counter-clockwise rotation determined by looking at the face of the gas turbine output shaft coupling.

Fuel Gas Compressor: A compressor used to raise the pressure of the fuel gas to permit its introduction into the combustor.

Fuel Pump (Liquid): A pump used to supply the pressure necessary to introduce and distribute the liquid fuel in the combustor.

Availability: Ratio of time unit is in use to total time or,

$$\frac{(\text{Total Installed Hours}) - (\text{Planned and Forced Outages})}{(\text{Total Installed Hours})}$$

Reliability: Ratio of time unit is in use according to plan, or

$$\frac{(\text{Total Installed Hours}) - (\text{Forced Outages})}{(\text{Total Installed Hours})}$$

CHAPTER I

Gas Turbine Components and Cycles

The simple cycle gas turbine is one of the least complicated machines yet developed for the production of pneumatic and shaft power. The engine operates through a continuous cycle which normally consists of a series of events, which are: compression of air taken from the atmosphere, increase of the air temperature by the constant pressure combustion of fuel, expansion of the hot gases through a turbine, and, finally, discharge of the gases to atmosphere—the whole being a continuous flow process. This process is shown schematically in Fig. 1–1. This cycle is called the simple cycle, as contrasted with cycles which use intercooling, reheating, exhaust heat recovery, and other modifications. It is the cycle which will be discussed first.

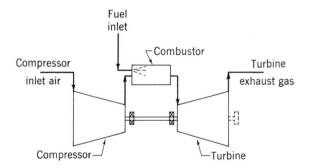

FIG. 1–1. Schematic diagram of simple, open-cycle, single-shaft gas turbine engine

FIG. 1–2. Multi-stage axial compressor assembly

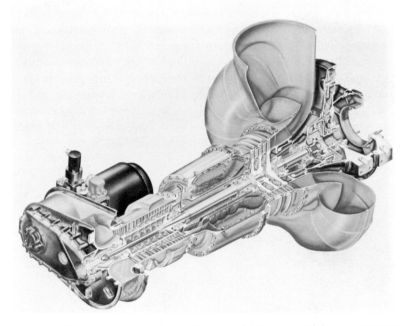

FIG. 1–3. Two shaft gas turbine that has an eight-stage axial-flow compressor
and a three-stage axial-flow turbine

Compressor

The compressor is the first basic mechanical element in the gas turbine cycle. There are two types of compressors being used in gas turbines at the present time. They are centrifugal compressors and axial flow compressors. Generally speaking, large gas turbines (1000 hp and higher) utilize multiple-stage axial flow compressors because of their ability to handle large volumes of air at high efficiency. In addition, axial flow compressors lend themselves easily to high pressure ratio machines.

Figure 1–2 illustrates a typical multi-stage axial compressor assembly and Fig. 1–3 shows a two-shaft gas turbine with an eight-stage axial flow compressor. Small gas turbine engines normally utilize one or two centrifugal compressors (see Fig. 1–13), although some utilize combination axial and centrifugal compressors. Centrifugal compressors tend to be more compact and less expensive to produce by pres-

FIG. 1–4.   Typical centrifugal compressor assemblies

ently established methods than axial compressors for small gas turbines. Further, the centrifugal compressor is less susceptible to damage from large foreign particles passing through the engine. Single-stage centrifugal compressors are used successfully in many small gas turbines. Impeller designs have developed to a point where good efficiencies are attainable at single stage compression ratios up to approximately 6:1. Higher performance, simple cycle gas turbines, however, require compressor pressure ratios greater than those attainable with a single-stage compressor impeller. In engines of this type, either two centrifugal stages are used or one centrifugal stage is used with one or more axial stages.

Figure 1–4 illustrates typical two-stage compressor impeller designs. Some loss in efficiency is experienced going from a single-stage to two-stage centrifugal compression due to the losses in the interstage passages.

Combustor

The combustor is the second basic component in the gas turbine cycle. The combustor must operate efficiently over a wide range of ambient conditions with widely varying rates of fuel flow from engine no-load to full rated load conditions.

In order to achieve complete combustion, a stoichiometric mixture of approximately 15 parts of air (by weight) to one part of fuel is required in the primary zone where the combustion occurs. However, the gas turbine engine requires approximately 70 to 80 parts of air (by weight) to one part of fuel in order to cool the combustion gases from approximately 3500 deg F to the permissible turbine inlet temperatures. Since a lean mixture is difficult to ignite and maintain at continuous combustion, it is for this reason that a stoichiometric mix-

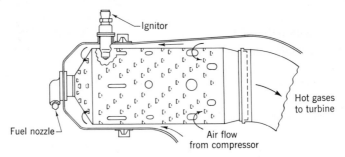

Fig. 1–5.   Combustion process in a reverse flow can-type compressor

ture must be achieved in what is referred to as the primary zone of the combustion chamber. The combustor zone into which air is admitted to quench the hot combustion gases is known as the secondary zone of the combustion chamber. Figure 1–5 shows the combination process of a reverse flow can-type combustor and Fig. 1–6 gives a cutaway view of a gas turbine employing 8 reverse-flow combustors, only one of which is shown at the upper right.

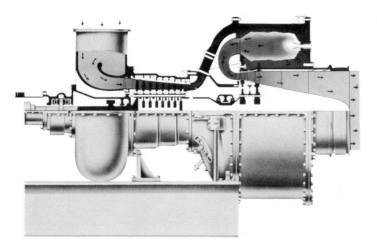

Fig. 1–6. Gas turbine employing eight reverse-flow combustors that has a two-stage axial-flow turbine driving an eight-stage axial compressor

Combustion efficiency is defined as the ratio of actual heat developed during combustion, from a given quantity of fuel, to the total equivalent heat of the same given quantity of fuel, flowing through the combustion chamber. Combustion efficiencies on the order of 96 to 99 percent are common in gas turbine engines. Poor combustion efficiency can, in part, be attributed to too large a quantity of primary or secondary air being admitted too soon which could result in incomplete combustion, with unburned fuel passing through the turbine. Any loss in combustion efficiency represents a direct loss in over-all engine thermal efficiency.

Two basic methods of injecting liquid fuel are used. In one system, fuel is injected into the combustion chamber through an atomizer or nozzle assembly as a fine mist and is burned in this form. In the other, known as the vaporizing type, fuel is metered into a tube which is surrounded by combustion gases. The hot tube and some hot air flowing through the tube evaporates the fuel, and the rich fuel air mix-

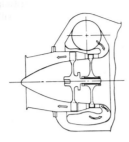
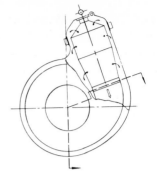

CANNULAR

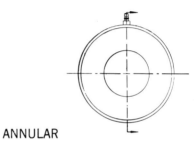

ANNULAR

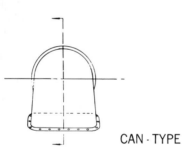

CAN - TYPE

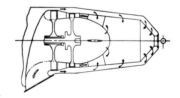

STRAIGHT THRU - FLOW

FIG. 1–7.   Four basic types of combustors

ture is discharged into the combustion zone where it is mixed with additional air and is burned. The most common method of injecting liquid fuel is by the atomizer or nozzle assembly.

The same basic combustion system is utilized when burning gaseous fuels. Combustors which perform satisfactorily on liquid fuels generally will operate without difficulty on gaseous fuels. The fuel system is the only basic section to be changed for conversion. A gas fuel nozzle is quite simple compared to its liquid fuel counterpart. The tip of the nozzle embodies several orifices which are sized and spaced to provide the necessary dispersion of the gas in the combustor. The basic requirement is to compress the gas to some nominal value above the engine compressor discharge pressure in order to admit the gas into the combustor.

The combustion process is normally initiated by a spark ignition system consisting of a high-energy capacitor discharge ignition unit, an ignition lead, and an ignitor plug. The ignition unit usually is energized only during the starting cycle. Thereafter, the combustion process is self-sustained by the stabilized flame front in the primary zone of the combustor.

Gas turbines may utilize single, double or multiple chambers to handle the combustion function. The choice in the matter is largely dictated by the space requirements of the application and beyond that it is mostly a matter of the designer's preference. Figure 1–7 illustrates four basic types of combustors. Aircraft turbines are normally equipped with the smaller multi-can type chambers that can be located around the engine periphery. The result is a reduction in overall space requirement and frontal area, which is a basic requirement for aircraft turbines. Industrial turbine designers not primarily concerned with frontal area or stringent space requirements usually base their final selection on other design problems such as combustion efficiency, pressure drop, balanced flow distribution and balanced temperature distribution across all sections of the chamber outlet. European designers have generally used single chambers except on aircraft turbines. Successful industrial turbine installations are in operation with all of the major combustion chamber configurations and the user need not be concerned about acceptance of a turbine because of this question.

Turbine

The third basic element in the gas turbine is the expansion turbine or power producing element of the engine. The pressurized hot gases from the combustion chamber provide the energy for the turbine. The temperature of the gases entering the turbine range from approximately 1200 to 1700 deg F under continuous full load operations for most commercial turbines presently on the market. This temperature range will be higher as time goes on due to improvements in materials and design techniques. The first part of each turbine stage is a nozzle assembly. The nozzles restrict, accelerate (an expansion process), and direct the flow into the turbine wheel. After passing through the nozzle and entering the rotor, the hot gas continues its expansion process through the turbine wheel blading and imparts rotative force to the turbine shaft. Approximately two-thirds of the total power developed by the turbine is used to drive the compressor and engine accessories. The remaining shaft horsepower is the useful output of the engine.

The expansion turbine may be of the axial flow type or radial type. The most widely used type in low pressure ratio small gas turbines is a single-stage, radial-inflow turbine (Fig. 1–8) in which the gases

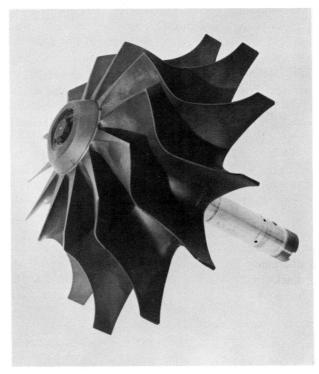

FIG. 1–8.   Typical radial in-flow, single-stage turbine assembly

flow from the wheel rim radially across the wheel and exhaust from the "eye" or center of the wheel. A single-stage, radial wheel generally is best suited for an engine with a pressure ratio of approximately 4:1. Above this pressure ratio, either a combination radial and axial or a two- or three-stage axial turbine assembly (Fig. 1–9) is utilized.

FIG. 1–9.   Typical axial flow, three-stage turbine assembly

Exhaust Heat Recovery Devices

For increased over-all engine efficiency, a turbine exhaust-to-compressor discharge heat exchanger can be added to recover some of the exhaust heat and thus reduce the amount of fuel that is required to produce a given output power. The heat exchanger can be either of two types—recuperator or regenerator. In a recuperator, the hot turbine exhaust gas flows on one side of the heat transfer surface and the cooler compressor discharge air flows in the other side. The regenerator alternately heats an intermediate substance such as layers of screen, stacks of finely corrugated metal, or porous ceramic in the turbine exhaust which in turn imparts heat to the compressor discharge air.

Figure 1–10 schematically illustrates a heat recovery cycle. In this cycle, heat is extracted from the turbine exhaust gases and added to the compressed air stream prior to its entry into the combustion chamber. Heat recovered in the heat exchanger permits reduc-

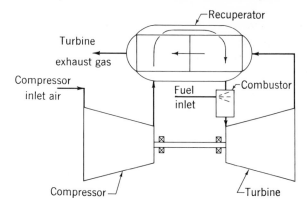

FIG. 1–10. Schematic diagram showing gas turbine exhaust heat recovery
cycle

tion of fuel input by approximately 25 to 50 percent depending on the
effectiveness of the heat exchanger. The weight and size of heat
exchangers depend directly on the heat exchanger effectiveness as
shown in Fig. 1–11.

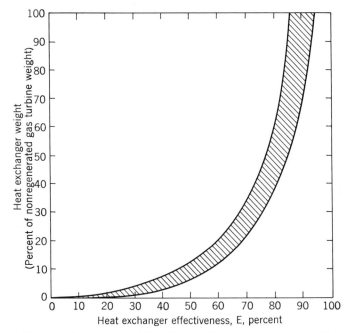

FIG. 1–11. Graph showing relationship of effectiveness versus weight of gas
turbine heat exchangers

The large increases in weight of the heat exchanger at high heat exchanger effectiveness makes somewhat more modest heat exchanger effectiveness attractive in many applications. For a particular engine, for example, a decrease in effectiveness from 85 to 60 percent would increase the specific fuel consumption approximately 15 percent but the heat exchanger weight would be reduced 60 percent. Regenerative turbines are not in extensive use today except in large, stationary, continuous duty application.

Reheaters and Intercoolers

The power of a given size turbine may be increased by means of reheaters and intercoolers. The use of intercoolers and/or reheaters can improve engine efficiency but only when they are used in conjunction with a recuperator or regenerator. This is done, however, at the expense of added complexity and cost. In the reheat cycle a second stage of heating is added between sections of the turbine to increase the temperature of the working fluid. An intercooler reduces the work of compression by removing the heat of compression between compressor stages.

Turbine Cycles

The majority of gas turbines in use today are of the simple, open cycle type. In the open cycle gas turbine there is no recirculation of the working fluid (air and combustion products) within the power plant, the inlet and exhaust being open to the atmosphere.

A closed cycle machine is one in which the working fluid is continuously recycled through the machine and does not come into physical contact with the combustion products. Heat is transferred from an external heat source to the working fluid of the cycle by heat transfer surface. This offers the advantage of a clean working fluid and use of a wide range of fuels. In the closed cycle engine the compressor inlet air pressure may be varied to control the weight of working fluid circulated without changing the compression ratio or temperatures. Thus, it is possible to operate over a wide load range at practically constant speed and efficiency. The major disadvantage of this cycle is the complexity and the resulting size and cost of the system. The closed cycle system is not found in general use and is more predominantly used in special applications involving large horsepower turbines.

Shaft Arrangement

One of the major classifications used to describe a basic gas turbine design has to do with the shaft arrangement of the power turbine. As described previously, the turbine extracts enough energy from the hot gases to drive the compressor and supplies additional shaft power to drive other accessory equipment. If all the turbine stages are on the same shaft as the compressor, the gas turbine is called a "single shaft" or "fixed shaft" turbine. This configuration is schematically illustrated in Fig. 1–1. The power turbine can be divided into two sections. The portion of this type of engine which has only the turbine stages required to drive the compressor on the same shaft as the compressor is called a gas producer turbine or a gas generator turbine. The turbine stages that supply the power to the driven turbine are put on a separate shaft. This type of turbine is called a "two-shaft" or "split-shaft" or "free turbine" engine, and is schematically and pictorially illustrated in Figs. 1–12 and 1–13, respectively.

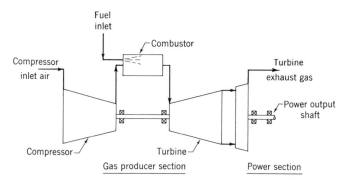

FIG. 1–12.   Schematic diagram of free turbine (two-shaft) engine

The decision of whether to use a single shaft or a two shaft engine is based more on the decision of the application engineer than the design choices mentioned previously for the basic elements of the gas turbine. In some instances, turbines of a given power rating required of a specific application may not be available in both single and two shaft versions. If so, of course, the engineer must evaluate the suitability of the available turbine for the application and decide whether or not a gas turbine is to be used. At the present time, however, there are some gas turbines on the market which can be supplied with either shaft arrangement. In those instances, the engineer must decide which

FIG. 1–13. Free-turbine engine with two horizontal combustors and a centrifugal compressor that is driven by a single-stage axial-flow high pressure turbine which exhausts to a single-stage axial-flow low-pressure free turbine

type of turbine has the characteristics which most nearly match those required by the driven equipment.

Generally speaking, the single shaft turbine is most applicable to constant speed applications, such as generator drives, and turbines of this type have been used successfully to drive pumps or compressors in installations where constant speed operation is satisfactory. Cost is one of the favorable aspects of the single shaft turbine. The selling price of the single shaft engine will usually be equal to or less than the same turbine in a two shaft model. This is due largely to the mechanical simplicity of the single shaft turbine and the consequent reduction of manufacturing cost.

Speed variation of a single shaft turbine requires a simple fuel control. As a result, the constant speed control response which is required for generator drive is more rapid for the single shaft turbine than the two shaft turbine. Single shaft turbine speed controls have been developed that can handle wide variations of load of an instantaneous nature and still maintain very close voltage and frequency tolerances at the generator terminals. Two shaft turbines can be equipped with governors that satisfactorily maintain generator speed during rapid load changes; however, there is an inherent time lag required for the gas generator section of the engine to respond to load variations, and this should be considered in the decision to purchase a two shaft turbine for generator drive applications.

The starting torque requirements for a given application should be thoroughly analyzed before making a decision regarding the selection of a single or two shaft turbine. It is not a problem that is beyond solution for either type of turbine, if thoroughly understood, but this understanding should be accomplished in the initial stages of any application analysis. The starter power and torque requirement will be greater for a single shaft turbine than a two shaft turbine due to the simple fact that the starting unit on a single shaft turbine has to start and accelerate the entire rotating mass of the engine and the driven equipment as well, while the starter of a two shaft turbine is required only to start and accelerate the gas generator section of the engine. As the gas generator comes up to speed it pressurizes the system and imposes some torque on the output or power turbine wheel. The power turbine will start to rotate when enough torque is imposed upon its blades. This output shaft rotation may begin at any point in the starting cycle when the torque is sufficient to overcome the driven load. This may happen after the gas generator is up to speed, and the combustor fires off and is operating at rated temperature. This would be comparable to a locked rotor starting situation. As far as the driven equipment is concerned, the two shaft turbine has torque characteristics very similar to those of a steam turbine, i. e., high breakaway or stall torque, and it can handle a driven load during startup without the requirement for high horsepower starting equipment.

The other consideration involved in comparing the starting requirements of single and two shaft turbines is the starting characteristics of the system served by the driven equipment. This factor is not so important in the starting of a generator unit but it does seriously affect the starting problem with pumps or compressors as the driven equipment. Some installations of pumps and compressors are such that the driven equipment can be started and brought up to speed in a vented or unloaded condition. Under these conditions the start-up problem of a pump or compressor installation will not be any more difficult than for a generator unit. In applications such as air conditioning, with reciprocating compressor drives, where the driven equipment is in a closed piping circuit, the starting equipment of a single-shaft turbine must not only handle the load of rotating and accelerating its own rotors but it must also carry a pumping load resulting from the speed of the driven compressor rotor in a closed circuit. This pumping load can be handled by installing a piping bypass around the compressor, isolating the compressor by closing suction and discharge block valves, or reducing the load by suction valve throttling. In any event, this problem must be recognized and disposed of if a single-shaft turbine is to be used on an installation involving the direct drive of a refrigeration compressor or any other item of equipment that must be started in a pressurized circuit under load.

The difference in output torque versus speed characteristics between single and two shaft turbines must also be considered by the application engineer. This is more significant in installations involving pumps and compressors. The speed flexibility of the two shaft turbine results in its being able to meet or exceed the speed-load requirements of all types of driven equipment. Some speed variation is possible with the fixed shaft engine and this speed range should be investigated before deciding on a particular type of turbine. Characteristic output shaft torque curves for a two shaft turbine and a single shaft turbine, are shown in Fig. 1–14.

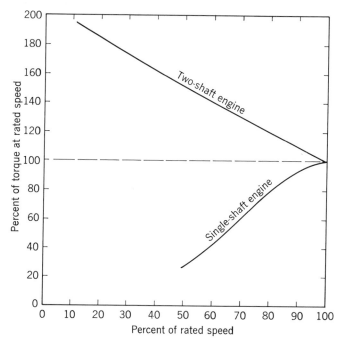

FIG. 1–14. Variation of torque with power turbine speed for single and two-shaft engines

Thrust Output Arrangement

The majority of large aircraft turbine engines that have been produced are of the thrust producing type. This type of engine is finding application where the engine acts as a hot gas generator which can then be used to drive a power turbine which can provide for shaft power extraction.

Bleed Air Output Arrangement

The majority of small gas turbines, particularly in the 200 to 300 horsepower size, are so designed that the total useful output of the engine is in the form of compressed air. This type of engine is commonly referred to as a "bleed-off" turbine. The compressor of the engine is in effect oversized in order to bleed off approximately 30 percent of the compressor throughflow. The air is bled off the compressor prior to entering the combustor and turbine. This type of engine was developed specifically for the purpose of providing a small lightweight source of compressed air for driving air turbine starters that are used for starting large turbojet and turboprop aircraft engines. By resizing the compressor and/or the combustor and turbine, the bleed-off engine can simultaneously provide bleed air and/or shaft power.

Shaft Output Arrangement

Shaft power gas turbine engines normally provide output speeds that range from approximately 1200 rpm to 6000 rpm. These speeds are provided by gear reduction as the turbine and compressors generally rotate at speeds that range from 40,000 to 60,000 rpm (for powers of about 50 to 200 hp), down to 3600 rpm (for some engines in the 10,000 to 30,000 hp class).

Performance

A characteristic full load output power curve for a shaft turbine engine for various compressor inlet air temperatures (ambient) is shown in Fig. 1–15. It can be noted from this curve that an appreciable change in output power occurs with changes in ambient tempera-

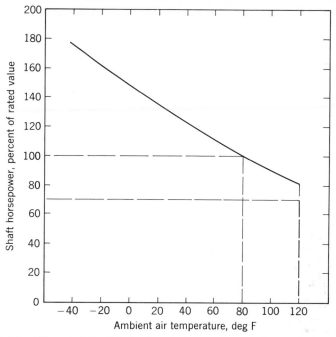

Fig. 1–15. Characteristic full load output power curve for a shaft turbine engine for various compressor inlet air temperatures (ambient)

ture. This temperature effect is much more pronounced with the gas turbine engine than with the internal combustion engine. In a reciprocating engine, power output varies inversely as the square root of the ratio of atmospheric air absolute temperatures. Thus, if the intake air temperature in a reciprocating engine increased from 50 to 115 deg F, the power output would decrease about 5 percent. This power reduction is due mainly to the decrease in engine mass flow (weight of air aspirated by the engine). In the case of the gas turbine, an increase in intake air temperature also decreases the mass flow through the compressor and turbine, but, in addition, the compressor pressure ratio also decreases. Second, as the turbine compressor inlet temperature is increased, the compressor discharge temperature is also increased and, as a result, less energy can be added by combustion to this less dense air to produce a given turbine inlet temperature. The over-all result is that as ambient temperature increases, the total power produced by the engine decreases owing to a lower mass flow and a lower pressure ratio. In a typical gas turbine, if the compressor inlet temperature were increased from 50 to 115 deg F, the power output would decrease about 30 percent.

The actual slope of the curve or variation of output power with ambient temperature will differ somewhat from turbine to turbine depending on the performance characteristics of each engine. The specific variation with temperature must be obtained from the turbine manufacturer.

Standard Rated Power

Power from a turbine depends on mass flow (pounds of air flow per unit of time) and adiabatic head. Adiabatic head is a measure of the energy in the air or gas available for expansion through the turbine. This expansion is analogous to the head on a water wheel and is measured in the same units as hydraulic head, namely, feet or foot-pounds per pound.

Adiabatic head depends on temperature and pressure ratio. With fixed temperatures and pressures, the power of a given turbine can be varied only by mass flow.

The effects of decreased ambient pressure (increased altitude) also have a pronounced effect on the gas turbine. This decrease in performance is again due to the lower density of the air, which results in lower mass flow through the engine.

Site Rated Power

Engine output power at altitude varies directly as the ratio of absolute atmospheric pressures. Thus, if a gas turbine power unit produces 100 hp at sea level (29.92 in. Hg. abs) on an 80 deg F day, it will deliver approximately 83 hp at 5000 feet altitude (24.89 in. Hg. abs) on an 80 deg F day.

Turbine engine performance such as compressor bleed-air flow, compressor bleed-air pressure, shaft horsepower, and fuel consumption all vary directly with changes in ambient absolute pressures. It is also significant that, since atmospheric temperature almost always decreases as altitude increases, the available power will not drop so fast as the barometric pressure.

To sum up, when determining what size of gas turbine engine will be required for a particular application keep in mind the point that the *extremes of ambient pressure and temperature in which the unit will be required to operate must be known* in addition to the estimated loss in the inlet and discharge ducts.

Normal Rated Power

Aircraft turbine manufacturers normally rate their gas turbine engines at sea level pressure (29.92 in. Hg. abs) and an inlet temperature of 59 deg F. Standard industrial ratings are at an altitude of 1000 feet (28.86 in. Hg. abs) and 80 deg F inlet air temperature. These ratings are based on no compressor inlet or turbine discharge losses measured at the engine inlet and exhaust flanges. *Normal rated power* is the net maximum continuous output of the engine. *Site rated power* is the stated power of the gas turbine when it is operated under specified conditions of compressor inlet temperatures, compressor inlet pressure, and gas turbine exhaust pressure. It is measured at or is referred to the output shaft of the gas turbine or to the generator terminals.

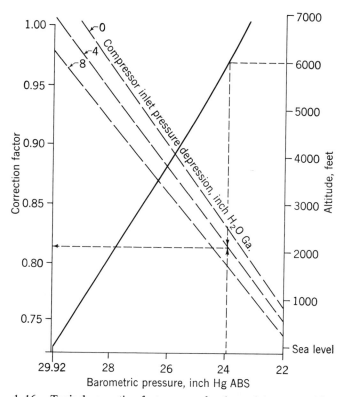

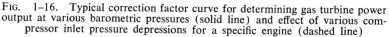

FIG.   1–16.   Typical correction factor curve for determining gas turbine power output at various barometric pressures (solid line) and effect of various compressor inlet pressure depressions for a specific engine (dashed line)

A typical correction curve that can be utilized for all gas turbines at various altitudes and zero compressor inlet losses is shown as the solid line in Fig. 1–16. This particular correction factor curve is based on a standard altitude of 1000 feet. In addition, the graph shows in dashed lines, the effect of compressor inlet or duct pressure drops for a particular engine at full load.

The turbine exhaust losses (back pressure) also have an appreciable effect on the performance of the engine. A 2-inch water column inlet loss will affect engine performance more than a 2-inch water column back pressure on the turbine. There is neither a single back pressure correction curve nor a single inlet pressure drop curve that will be applicable to all gas turbines as effect of the degree of back pressure and of inlet depression varies with different engines. This information must be obtained from the turbine manufacturer.

Characteristic performance curves for a *simple open cycle two shaft engine,* including maximum engine output power, torque, and variations in specific fuel consumption, for various output shaft speeds, are given in Fig. 1–17. The curves are general in nature and will vary

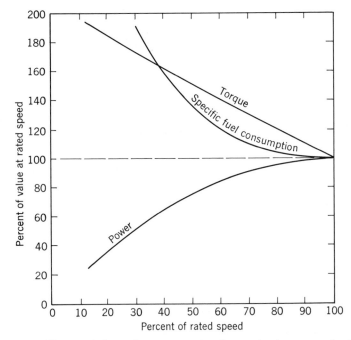

Fig. 1–17.   Characteristic performance curves for a simple open-cycle two-shaft engine

somewhat depending on the particular engine.   Similar characteristic performance curves for a *simple, open-cycle, single-shaft engine,* showing maximum output power and torque over a limited output speed range, appear in Fig. 1–18.   As with Fig. 1–17, the curves in Fig.

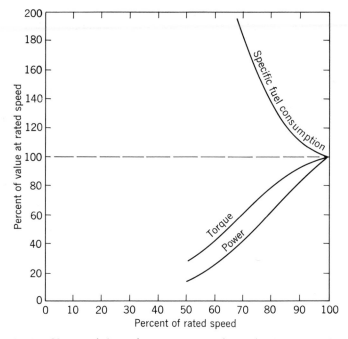

FIG. 1–18.   Characteristic performance curves for a simple open-cycle single-shaft engine

1–18 reflect only the general characteristics of the engine and in detail will vary somewhat depending on the particular design.   In both cases the turbine manufacturer should be consulted for the characteristics of a particular model.

Turbine Performance Characteristics

Possible methods of improving thermal efficiency of the gas turbine include (1) increasing turbine inlet temperature, (2) increasing compressor pressure ratio within a certain range, (3) increasing component efficiencies, and (4) use of compressor intercoolers and exhaust gas heat exchangers.

For a given gas-generator-turbine inlet temperature, thermal efficiency and specific power (horsepower per pound of engine air flow per second) will increase with an increase in compressor pressure ratio up to a peak value and then will steadily decrease with further increases in pressure ratio. Conversely, for a given compressor pressure ratio, thermal efficiency and engine specific power will increase with an increase in gas-generator-turbine inlet temperature.

If turbine inlet temperatures of the order of 2400 deg F could be achieved, it would be possible to obtain simple cycle gas turbine engine efficiencies comparable to those of diesel engines. The gas turbine engine power characteristics would then approach the characteristics of the reciprocating internal combustion engine; that is, the same horsepower could be produced with a substantial decrease in engine air flow. Therefore, it appears that the best way to achieve higher over-all efficiency of the small gas turbine engine is to increase turbine inlet temperatures. It is believed that, in order to attain the higher turbine temperatures, considerable effort should be expended

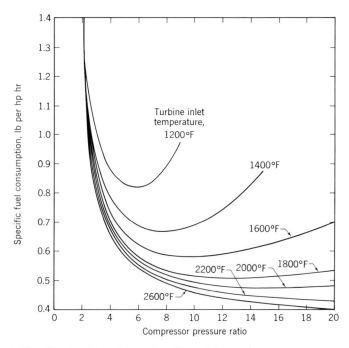

Fig. 1–19. Graph which shows the effect of increasing gas-generator-turbine inlet temperature on specific fuel consumption at various compressor pressure ratios

in the future to develop new techniques, such as turbine wheel cooling, in addition to the development of new turbine materials.

The effect of increasing gas-generator-turbine inlet temperature on specific fuel consumption at various compressor pressure ratios is illustrated in Fig. 1–19.   In the next few years a gradual rise in turbine temperatures to approximately 1800 deg F can be expected.   Although this will permit a modest reduction in specific fuel consumption, the higher temperature will result in a much higher engine specific power. For example, an engine of the same physical size (same engine air flow) having a compressor pressure ratio of 6:1 can produce approximately 30 percent more power when operating at a turbine inlet temperature of 1800 deg F than one with a turbine inlet temperature of 1600 deg F.   The effect of increasing turbine inlet temperature on engine specific power at various compressor pressure ratios is shown in Fig. 1–20.

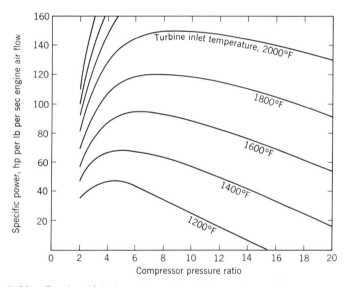

Fig. 1–20.   Graph which shows the effect of increasing turbine inlet temperature on engine specific power at various compressor pressure ratios

Variation of engine component efficiencies will affect the precise shape of the curves in Figs. 1–19 and 1–20.   However, the curves shown illustrate the general relationship of compressor pressure ratio and turbine inlet temperature to engine thermal efficiency.

High engine component efficiencies are normally found in large gas turbine engines. These efficiencies, especially those of the compressor and turbine components, gradually reduce as the engine size or power rating is reduced. Gas turbine parasitic power losses such as heat loss through walls, windage losses, bearing and seal losses, and fuel and oil pump losses, are not reduced proportionally with diminishing design power and so become more significant as the engine design power is reduced. Also, aerodynamic losses become fractionally larger, since leading and trailing edges (as well as surface finishes and clearances) cannot be scaled down directly in reducing gas turbine power and size.

CHAPTER 2

Gas Turbine Accessories

Gas turbine accessories are those parts of the engine not directly involved in the production and handling of the engine's useful power output. They do perform auxiliary services essential to the production, control, and handling of the engine's useful power output. Even the simplest gas turbine engine cycle involves the use of many small and separately manufactured accessories. Most of them are established as possessing a high degree of dependability by a very respectable length of development, testing, and field service. Yet they tend to be small, complex mechanisms. This, together with the number of accessories involved per engine, requires that full attention be given to the selection and integration of accessories to provide an engine of maximum reliability.

Fuel Systems—General

The fuel system consists of piping, manifolding, and in some instances, one or more pumps as required to deliver fuel to the combustor at a sufficient pressure to perform satisfactory injection. Elements of the control system such as shut-off valves, and regulators will be found in the fuel system between engine inlet and combustor.

Gas Fuel Systems

The pressure required to inject a gaseous fuel is essentially compressor discharge pressure plus the pressure losses in the control system and manifolds. A gaseous fuel injector usually consists of a tube with holes in it; the pressure drop across this injector is very small. The compressor pressure ratio of the engine determines the fuel pressure required, as shown in Fig. 2–1. The engine gas supply pressure shown on the upper curve in Fig. 2–1 is that which would be required at the fuel compressor discharge or at an engine inlet pressure regulating valve in the instance where supply pressure is sufficiently high.

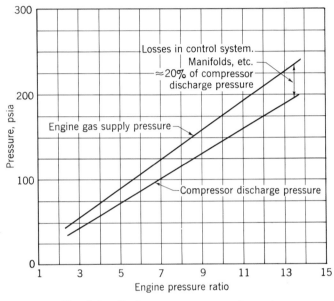

FIG. 2–1.   Fuel pump pressure requirement

Several factors affect the compressor power requirement for a gaseous fuel. Some of the factors are compressor efficiency, compressor compression ratio, gas main supply pressure, and heating value of the fuel. The effects of compressor efficiency, compression ratio, and gas main supply pressure on pump power requirements are shown in Fig. 2–2, which is based on a fuel heating value of 1000 Btu per cubic foot. A correction factor for fuels having other heating values is shown in Fig. 2–3.

Liquid Fuel Systems

The primary requirement for a liquid fuel system is that it have sufficient pressure to permit a pressure drop across the injector which is

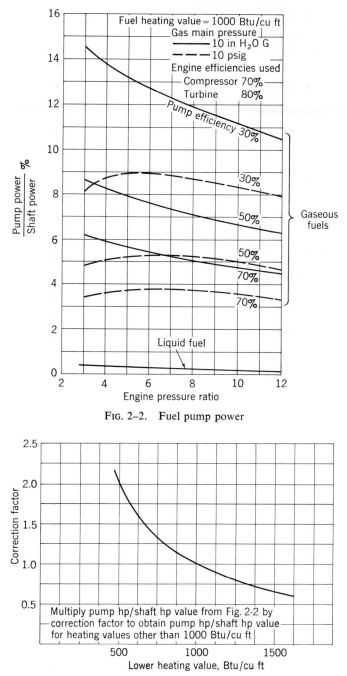

FIG. 2–2. Fuel pump power

FIG. 2–3. Effect of gas heating value on pump power

great enough to atomize the fuel. Obviously, the discharge pressure must be greater than that in the combustor or injection cannot be accomplished. The injector is usually an atomizing continuous spray nozzle. The pressure requirement for atomization varies depending on fuel viscosity and surface tension. Even though some liquid fuel systems require 500 to 1000 psi, the pump power requirements are low, as shown in the bottom curve of Fig. 2–2. The fuel pump is often an integral part of the control system.

Dual Fuel System

The primary fuel for a dual fuel engine is usually either natural gas or some process or waste gas, these being the least expensive fuels. Use of a second fuel, storable on the premises, most often is dictated by a requirement for emergency operation or by an interruptible service gas supply contract. The secondary fuel is usually a liquid fuel stored in tanks. The fuel and combustion system can be arranged so that transfer from the primary to secondary fuel is accomplished under load. This system of providing transfer under load may be complex, essentially involving two complete fuel systems, each having its fuel control devices continually in operation, and a combined fuel nozzle which can be used for either fuel. When the transfer is to be automatic, a switch to sense falling primary fuel supply pressure and a primary fuel storage volume in the pipe or other device sufficient to hold the pressure up until the secondary fuel reaches the combustor must be incorporated in the installation.

If interruption of service is permissible or can be scheduled, a somewhat simpler system can be used. The engine is stopped, the fuel nozzles changed, the governor reconnected for the secondary fuel, and the engine restarted. The changeover can usually be accomplished in a period ranging from 30 minutes to eight hours depending on design. Whether the change be manual or automatic, no change is necessary to either the engine or combustion chambers.

Starting Controls

The sequence of events required to start, run, load, and shut down a gas turbine can be controlled manually but is usually handled automatically. Large engines of over 2000 hp are ordinarily supplied with a means to furnish oil pressure before the cranking cycle is started.

After cranking has started, and a sufficient speed has been reached, the ignition system is energized and fuel is admitted to the combustor to start combustion. The starter continues to assist the engine, usually until it attains 30 to 40 percent of full speed, beyond which the engine is capable of continuing the start under its own power. As a rule, ignition is continued until the end of starter assist when the engine is then self-sustaining. In the event of a fast start, on the order of 20 seconds or less to idle speed, it is good practice to add approximately five seconds of holding with fuel off at or near light off speed for purging purposes before ignition is supplied.

Acceleration and Shut-Down Controls

Acceleration after light off is controlled by an acceleration limiter which schedules fuel to provide an acceleration rate within turbine design limits. The speed governor assumes control near full speed conditions and provides fuel corrections as needed to maintain turbine speed under varying load. A shut down signal supplied either manually or by any one of several protective devices will cause the fuel

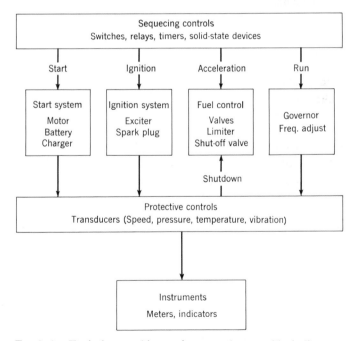

Fig. 2–4. Typical gas turbine engine control system block diagram

valve to be closed, thus stopping the engine. The components of such an elemental control system are shown graphically in Fig. 2–4.

Optional Controls

Depending upon the application to which the gas turbine is put, control systems of various degrees of complexity may be used. Existing engineering design of complex systems is sufficiently developed in all areas to provide nearly any function desired. As a rule it is more difficult and expensive to satisfy extremes of performance than extremes of complexity. For instance, a requirement for 0.1% frequency regulation in a driven alternator may be more difficult to obtain reliably than the control necessary to operate several alternators in parallel.

Most sequencing controls of an automatic nature are accomplished by electro-mechanical devices, such as relays, contractors, stepping switches, and timers. Depending upon the application, purely electronic equipment, such as magnetic amplifiers, semi-conductor devices, or electron tubes, may be used to provide complete or partial control of gas turbine engines and their driven alternators.

Governor

The operation of a gas turbine engine generally requires automatic fuel regulation for both starting and normal operation. Both functions may be performed by the governor or a separate acceleration limiter may be used for starting. Fuel control systems vary considerably depending upon a number of factors, such as degree of automation desired, closeness of speed regulation, operating characteristics of the particular engine, environmental considerations, and cost.

A typical fuel control or governing system is illustrated schematically in Fig. 2–5, which represents, more or less, a minimum fuel control system for a natural gas burning turbine engine. The fuel preferably is supplied from a source of sufficient capacity and pressure to meet the requirements of the particular engine without additional compression. Gas fuel compression power requirements are appreciable, as indicated by Fig. 2–2. A two position shut-off valve admits the fuel to the pressure regulator which meters the fuel as required. The engine is started and accelerated to governed speed with the acceleration fuel flow scheduled as indicated in Fig. 2–6. The regulator

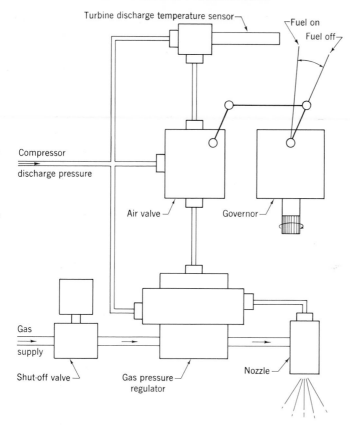

FIG. 2–5. Typical fuel control or governing system

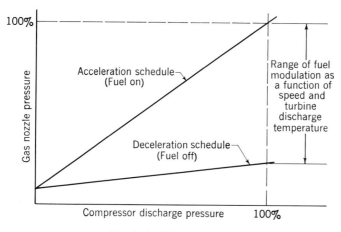

FIG. 2–6. Fuel schedule

schedules the gas nozzle pressure to a fixed ratio of the engine compressor discharge pressure. The gas nozzle area constitutes the metering area and thus fixes the fuel schedule. Either the speed governor or the turbine discharge temperature sensor can lower the schedule in order to regulate speed or to limit the turbine discharge temperature to that preset value corresponding with full load. The lower limit of the scheduled gas nozzle pressure allows the engine to decelerate under no load conditions but is maintained at a level sufficient to prevent flame out under any operating condition.

This basic system can be altered or added to as required. The governor itself can be any of several commercially available types of governors such as a simple droop type, an isochronous type, or a load sensing governor.

The system can be applied either to single or two shaft engines. In use with a two shaft engine, the addition of a power turbine governor to control power turbine speed will be required to regulate the fuel flow.

Protective Controls

Certain overload conditions or malfunctions of a gas turbine engine can be monitored to prevent possible destruction or damage to the engine. To provide this protection, certain basic protective devices are generally included with all gas turbine engines. The limits at which such controls operate may vary with engine application. Operation of the devices usually results in an engine shut-down and an alarm indication. Usual practice is to maintain alarm indication and control lockout to prevent restart until a deliberate alarm reset has been made.

The following protective controls are usually supplied with an engine:

Engine Overspeed: This control provides a means of detecting speeds approaching safety limits of the engine.

Temperature: Turbine inlet temperature is the physical quantity for which protection is desired but exhaust temperatures are more easily measured and are directly related to inlet temperatures.

Low Lubrication Oil Pressure

High Lubrication Oil Temperature

Flame Detection: Two conditions exist where it is important to know that combustion is proceeding normally in order to prevent damage to the engine.

a. *Light Off.* In starting, fuel valves are open and ignition is started and the fuel valve is opened. If the fuel fails to ignite, an explosive amount of fuel may soon accumulate and present a hazard. A light off detection method will usually be provided which shuts off the fuel supply if combustion does not occur within a very short time after fuel is admitted.

b. *Flame Out.* If a loss of combustion occurs during turbine engine operation, the same hazardous condition will arise as in failure to light off and the fuel supply must be shut off quickly. While the engine will lose power immediately, rotational energy will continue to provide fuel pressure for a short period.

Vibration: Any abnormal operation or malfunction which causes an unbalance in the rotating parts of a turbine engine or unstable combustion will cause a vibration level higher than normal for the engine.

Fuel Underpressure: Low fuel pressure either momentary or sporadic could result in erratic operation and hazardous conditions. A pressure operated switch is usually included in the protective controls to shut down the gas turbine in the event that fuel pressure falls below a safe level.

Instrumentation

The following minimum instrumentation is usually included with a gas turbine engine for installation and checkout purposes:

Speed: The usual engine speed indication is provided by a tachometer generator and indicator set using a small permanent magnet driven by the engine.

Inlet Temperatures: Knowledge of inlet temperature frequently is of use during operation and monitoring of an engine. It is essential for manual throttle operation.

Event Counter and Hourmeter: The engine manufacturer usually includes one or two devices for counting the number of starts and the total engine operating hours as an aid in establishing warranty periods and to provide a reliable record for maintenance schedules.

Lubrication System

The function of the lubrication system is to lubricate and cool bearings and gears, whether the engine uses journal bearings throughout, anti-friction bearings throughout, or a mixture of the two. Large engines with heavy rotating components on sleeve bearings require that lubrication pumps be driven separately from the engine. This is to provide the full lubrication pressure from start of rotation to standstill after shutdown. Smaller engines, particularly those with anti-friction bearings, use a single engine-driven lubrication pump. Some large engines use a combination of engine-driven and separate electric motor or steam turbine driven lubrication pumps. Oil reservoirs may be integrated with the engine or can be entirely separate. A common separate reservoir for several engines can be used. The latter arrangement is not to be recommended due to the possibility of transfer of contaminants from one engine to all of the others sharing the lubrication system.

In cold surroundings, an oil pre-start heater is useful. Depending upon the engine design, a separate oil cooler may or may not be required. If a water cooled oil cooler is used, the oil side pressure should be higher than the water side pressure and the cooler arranged so that the engine will shut down due to low oil pressure or level in the event of cooler oil leakage. Use of one of the many commercially available oil filters is an economical insurance measure. On larger installations, parallel filter systems should be used with separate pressure drop measurement and shut off provisions made to detect the need for filter service and to permit it under load.

Anti-Icing System

In those instances where situations arise when it is impossible to avoid the combination of moisture, cool air, and a sufficient velocity and/or pressure drop in the inlet duct which will permit condensation and freezing of moisture from inlet air of very high relative humidity, anti-icing systems will be required.

Remedies are available in the form of local heating of the surface on which ice tends to form or heating of the entire inlet air supply to approximately 40 deg F. The latter method is particularly attractive in that turbine engines realize maximum efficiency at design conditions of speed and inlet temperature. Although inlet air below design temperature (60 to 80 deg F) allows an engine of a fixed size and speed to develop greater than design power (due to increased inlet air density), the efficiency is adversely affected. If anti-icing is required, automatic initiation is recommended with sufficient overlap into non-icing conditions of temperature, humidity, and pressure drop to insure prevention of ice formation rather than melting of ice after formation has started.

Bleed Air Control

In aircraft, bleed air is used for heating and air conditioning units. The dual axial compressor engines usually have three separate air bleed systems: high pressure, low pressure, and overboard bleeds. The high and low systems are used to drive aircraft and engine components or accessories, while the overboard bleed is required to preclude compressor instability. The high pressure compressor air is also used to anti-ice the engine air inlet and inlet duct.

Intercompressor bleed air is presently being used in industrial applications to provide limited shop air to support equipment and a small air motor.

Starter Systems

The function of the starter system is to accelerate the turbine to a speed sufficient that it will be able to complete the start on its own power. Unlike the compression ignition engine, which may require only a few revolutions of cranking, the gas turbine engine must be cranked to 10 or 20 percent speed before it will sustain itself at all, and to between 30 and 40 percent speed to complete the start within reasonable time and temperature limits. This is because the compressor and the turbine components of the engine are designed to operate efficiently at high speed where their power levels are high; consequently, at low speeds, their efficiencies are low.

The several different types of starting systems together with their advantages, disadvantages, and limitations are included in the following list.

1. *Electric.* An electric starting system consists of a motor, battery, battery charging system, and a means of connecting and disconnecting the motor and batteries.

a. Motor: The high starting torque of a DC motor qualifies it as a good gas turbine starting means. In some instances, an AC motor may prove satisfactory. Where engine mounted size and weight are of importance, a DC motor is generally used.

b. *Motor-Generator:* A DC motor requires a DC power source to drive it, usually a battery. It is common to use the motor as a generator, after the engine starts, to recharge the battery, and for other purposes. This usage generally requires a larger motor than if it were used only for starting, since the motor-generator must be rated for continuous duty while a starter is subject only to intermittent duty. The motor-generator also requires a voltage regulating system.

c. *Batteries and Chargers:* Both lead-acid and nickel-cadmium batteries are used for gas turbine applications. Usually lead-acid batteries are specified because of lower cost but where temperatures below approximately −30 deg F are encountered, nickel-cadmium batteries are considered superior. The most common battery voltage is 28 volts, although other voltages can be used.

Battery chargers vary from simple transformer rectifier units which provide an unregulated voltage to more sophisticated chargers which sense battery charge status, battery temperature, and provide a regulated and limited current for charging.

2. *Engine.* Reciprocating engines frequently are used to crank large gas turbine engines, especially those used in remote locations. They require use of a torque converter or other hydraulic transmission to supply the necessary high torque to the cranked engine from standstill until it has reached a self-sustaining speed.

3. *High Pressure Impingement:* Gas turbine engines can be started by high pressure air supplied to a special set of nozzles. The nozzle arrangement causes the air to impinge upon the turbine blades, setting the turbine and compressor in motion and developing sufficient rotational speed to effect a start. Such a system offers simplicity of the starting system at the expense of some complication of the engine turbine. It also requires a greater amount of compressed air energy to accomplish a start than would be required by a more efficient reciprocating or air motor.

4. *Hydraulic:* A hydraulic starter is used in gas turbine engine starting primarily for flexibility. For example, a single power supply such as a small reciprocating engine or an electric motor or a running gas turbine engine can supply pressure to a central system from which any of several engines might be started by hydraulic start motors. In this respect, hydraulic starters resemble electricity for starting purposes. However, the hydraulic starting system is more flexible than the electric system. By use of reservoirs, variable displacement motors, or pump motors, the torque can be held

virtually constant from initiation of cranking to assist speed or tailored to fit the power available to the cranking torque requirement.

5. *Hand Crank:* Direct hand cranking of gas turbine engines is limited to engine output powers in the range of 50 to 100 horsepower. A 50 hp engine might be hand cranked by a sturdy man at an ambient temperature as low as -65 deg F while 0 deg F is about the limit for one man hand cranking of a 100 hp output engine. Higher output power engines can be started by stored manual energy, as in a flywheel or in a hydraulic reservoir.

6. *Compressed Air or Gas:* Usable sources of compressed air or gas for gas turbine engine starting are high pressure natural gas, plant compressed air, or high pressure air bled from either an intermediate stage or a final stage of an operating gas turbine. Bottled gas, such as nitrogen, and steam, may also be considered in the same category as suitable for gas turbine engine starting. All may be used in a small reciprocating or rotary starting motor or in a direct injection system. Shut off and usually pressure control valves are required in all instances.

CHAPTER 3

Fuels

Three types of fuels are commonly used by gas turbines—natural gas, liquified petroleum gas, and liquid fuels. Solid fuels can also be used.

Natural Gas

Natural gas is the ideal fuel for gas turbine operation in many respects. It requires no vaporization prior to burning as do liquid or solid fuels. It is clean and has no contaminants to cause blade deposits, corrosion or erosion. It produces no air pollutants or exhaust gas impurities when burned properly. Natural gas does not require storage facilities or inventory expense. Normally, it is burned before payment is required and is available in most sections of the United States at competitive prices.

However, natural gas is not available normally from the gas utility at pressures sufficiently high to be used directly in the turbine. Thus, a gas pressure booster generally is required and some power is needed to operate this booster, either directly from the turbine shaft or from another source. Many turbine manufacturers are developing integral gas pressure boosters for use with their gas turbines. Separate gas compressors have been used by industry for many years for other purposes.

The principal constituent of natural gas is methane, with small percentage quantities of ethane and less common gases forming the remainder. Natural gas chemical analyses vary somewhat depending upon the source of supply. The turbine manufacturer should be supplied with an analysis for the gas to be used in a specific application. This analysis is available from the utility which will be supplying gas service. Other gases may be considered for turbine fuel. Table 3–1 gives the natural gas analysis for 48 cities.

Natural gas is generally rated and sold at the high or gross heating value. The gas turbine, however, recognizes only the low or net heating value in the development of power. The difference is a function of the combustion process which combines hydrogen, a constituent of all hydrocarbon fuels, with oxygen in the burning process to form water. This water is vaporized during combustion and passes out with the exhaust gases, thus absorbing heat energy in the evaporative process which cannot be put to work. This is the reason that only the net heating value of natural gas is meaningful in fuel consumption versus horsepower calculations. The carbon portion of the fuel combines with oxygen without producing water and all heat so produced is theoretically available to the turbine. The so-called hydrogen loss averages about 8% but may amount to 10%.

Other factors affecting gas flow and fuel consumption are specific gravity (natural gas is lighter than air), water vapor entrained with delivered gas (negligible in utility furnished natural gas), temperature, and pressure.

Sulfur bearing natural gas which has not been processed may be supplied for turbine fuel in oil or gas field operation. Special provision to utilize this fuel may be required of the turbine manufacturer because of the corrosive qualities of sulfur, a constituent not usually found in utility-supplied natural gas.

Liquefied Petroleum Gas

Liquefied petroleum gases (LPG) such as propane and butane are excellent fuels for gas turbine use. The burning characteristics are practically identical to those of natural gas. At normal temperatures LPG will change from liquid to a gaseous state unless contained under pressure in the neighborhood of 100 psig depending on the composition of the fuel. In the gaseous state LPG is heavier than air and for this reason special precautions must be taken to ventilate or eliminate depressed areas where leaking gases might accumulate. LPG is denser than natural gas and contains more thermal energy

Table 3–I. Natural Gas Distributed in Various Cities in the United States*

(Surveyed by A.G.A. in the fall of 1962)

No.	City	Components of gas, per cent by volume									Heat. value,† Btu/cu ft	Sp gr
		Methane	Ethane	Propane	Butanes	Pentanes	Hexanes plus	CO_2	N_2	Miscel.		
1	Abilene, Tex.	73.52	13.23	4.35	0.56	0.06	0.11	0.16	8.01	...	1121	0.710
2	Akron, Ohio	93.30	3.49	0.69	.18	.04	.00	0.50	1.80	...	1037	.600
3	Albuquerque, N. M.	86.10	9.49	2.34	.44	.08	.03	1.02	0.50	...	1120	.646
4	Atlanta, Ga.	93.42	2.80	0.65	.33	.12	.10	1.38	1.20	...	1031	.604
5	Baltimore, Md.	94.40	3.40	.60	.50	.00	.00	0.60	0.50	...	1051	.590
6	Birmingham, Ala.	93.14	2.50	.67	.32	.12	.05	1.06	2.14	...	1024	.599
7	Boston, Mass.	93.51	3.82	.93	.28	.07	.06	0.94	0.39	...	1057	.604
8	Brooklyn, N. Y.	94.52	3.29	0.73	.26	.10	.09	0.70	0.31	...	1049	.595
9	Butte, Mont.	87.38	3.02	1.09	.11	.06	.09	1.98	6.36	...	1000	.610
10	Canton, Ohio	93.30	3.49	0.69	.18	.04	.00	0.50	1.80	...	1037	.600
11	Cheyenne, Wyo.	91.00	4.73	1.20	.30	.06	.04	1.86	0.81	...	1060	.610
12	Cincinnati, Ohio	94.25	3.98	0.57	.16	.03	.03	0.68	0.30	...	1031	.591
13	Cleveland, Ohio	93.30	3.49	.69	.18	.04	.00	.50	1.80	...	1037	.600
14	Columbus, Ohio	93.54	3.58	0.66	.22	.06	.03	.85	1.11	...	1028	.597
15	Dallas, Tex.	86.30	7.25	2.78	.48	.07	.03	.63	2.47	...	1093	.641
16	Denver, Colo.	81.11	6.01	2.10	.57	.17	.03	.42	9.19	...	1011	.659
17	Des Moines, Iowa	80.38	6.39	2.46	.61	.08	.03	.20	9.53	0.32 He	1012	.669
18	Detroit, Mich.	89.92	4.21	1.34	.34	.09	.01	.59	3.30	.20 He	1016	.616
19	El Paso, Tex.	86.92	7.95	2.16	.16	.00	.00	.04	2.72	.05 He	1082	.630
20	Ft. Worth, Tex.	85.27	8.43	2.98	.62	.09	.04	.27	2.30	...	1115	.649
21	Houston, Tex.‡	92.50	4.80	2.00	.30	...	...	.27	0.13	...	1031	.623
22	Kansas City, Mo.	72.79	6.42	2.91	.50	.06	Trace	0.22	17.10	...	945	.695
23	Little Rock, Ark.	94.00	3.00	0.50	.20	.20	...	1.00	1.10	...	1035	.590

No.	City											
24	Los Angeles, Calif.	86.50	8.00	1.90	.30	.10	.10	0.50	2.60		1084	.638
25	Louisville, Ky.	94.05	3.41	0.40	.13	.05	.09	1.20	0.67		1034	.596
26	Memphis, Tenn.	92.50	4.37	0.62	.18	.07	.10	1.60	0.56		1044	.608
27	Milwaukee, Wis.	89.01	5.19	1.89	.66	.44	.02	0.00	2.73	.06 He	1051	.627
28	New Orleans, La.	93.75	3.16	1.36	.65	.66	.00	.42	0.00		1072	.612
29	New York City	94.52	3.29	0.73	.26	.10	.09	.70	0.31		1049	.595
30	Oklahoma City, Okla.	89.57	6.31	1.36	.36	.00	.00	.13	2.06		1080	.615
31	Omaha, Neb.	80.46	6.30	2.59	.68	.09	.05	.17	9.32	.21 O_2	1020	.669
32	Parkersburg, W. Va.	94.50	3.39	0.68	.12	.07	.03	.67	0.41	.34 He	1049	.592
33	Phoenix, Ariz.	87.37	8.11	2.26	.13	.00	.00	.61	1.37	.01 O_2	1071	.633
34	Pittsburgh, Pa.	94.03	3.58	0.79	.28	.07	.04	.80	0.40		1051	.595
35	Providence, R. I.	93.05	4.01	1.02	.34	.08	.08	1.00	0.42	.01 O_2	1057	.601
36	Provo, Utah	91.40	3.95	0.84	0.39	.03	.01	.52	2.86		1032	.605
37	Pueblo, Colo.	73.86	5.71	3.20	1.34	.14	.06	.13	15.26		980	.706
38	Rapid City, S. D.	90.60	7.20	0.82	0.19	.03	.03	.18	0.93	.02 He	1077	.607
39	St. Louis, Mo.	93.32	4.17	0.69	.19	.05		.98	0.61			
40	Salt Lake City, Utah	91.17	5.29	1.69	.55	.16	.03	.29	0.82		1082	.614
41	San Diego, Calif.	86.85	8.37	1.86	.15	.00	.00	.41	2.32	.04 He	1079	.643
42	San Francisco, Calif.	88.69	7.01	1.93	.28	.03	.00	.62	1.43	.01 He	1086	.624
43	Toledo, Ohio	93.54	3.58	0.66	.22	.06	.03	.85	1.11		1028	.597
44	Tulsa, Okla.	86.29	8.36	1.45	.18	.14	.01	.23	2.95	.39 O_2	1086	.630
45	Waco, Tex.	93.48	2.57	0.89	.43	.17	.11	1.69	0.66		1042	.607
46	Washington, D. C.	95.15	2.84	0.63	.24	.05	.05	.62	0.42		1042	.586
47	Wichita, Kan.	79.62	6.40	1.42	1.12	.48	.14	.10	10.62	0.10 O_2	1051	.660
48	Youngstown, Ohio	93.30	3.49	0.69	0.18	.04	0.00	0.50	1.80		1037	0.600

* Average analyses obtained from the operating utility company(s) supplying the city; the gas supply may vary considerably from these data—especially where more than one pipeline supplies the city. Also, as new supplies may be received from other sources, the analyses may change. Peak shaving (if used) is not accounted for in these data.

† Gross or higher heating value at 30 in. Hg, 60 F, dry. To convert to a saturated basis deduct 1.73 per cent; i.e., 17.3 from 1000, 19 from 1100.

‡ 1954 data.

Taken from the forthcoming Gas Engineers Handbook of the American Gas Association.

per cubic foot. Orifices are smaller and piping requirements are less than needed for natural gas. LPG usually costs more than natural gas for the same quantity of heat. It also may be blended with air in a proportional mixing device to produce a mixture which is compatible and interchangeable in the same burner utilizing natural gas. Properties of commercial LPG are listed in Table 3–2.

Table 3–2. Properties and Analyses of Commercial Liquefied Petroleum Gases

Properties and Analyses	Type of Gas			
	Propane (Natural Gas)	Propane (Refinery Gas)	Butane (Natural Gas)	Butane (Refinery Gas)
Specific gravity	1.55	1.77	2.04	2.00
Heat value, gross Btu per cu ft	2558	2504	3210	3184
Heat value, net, Btu per cu ft	2358	2316	2961	2935
Gross Btu per cu ft standard air	107.5	108.0	104.8	106.1
Cu ft air req'd per cu ft gas	23.8	23.2	30.6	30.0
Analysis in Per-Cent by Volume				
C_2H_6	2.2	2.0	—	—
C_3H_8	97.3	72.9	6.0	5.0
C_4H_{10}	0.5	0.8	{ 70.7 n- { 23.3 iso-	{ 50.1 n- { 16.5 iso-
C_3H_6	—	24.3	—	—
C_4H_8	—	—	—	28.3

LPG can be stored and pumped as a liquid. Storage facilities are costly, however, because pressure vessels are recommended and special physical clearances usually are required by local fire regulations. In some gas turbine systems LPG can be vaporized, controlled, and admitted as a gas without requiring a fuel pump. This permits an ideal situation for combustion. At low temperatures LPG is difficult to vaporize and auxiliary heat is required.

To take advantage of the lowest natural gas rates available in many areas, gas turbines may be equipped to burn an alternate fuel. Many gas utilities offer interruptible gas service at low rates, provided the customer can switch to a standby fuel at the utility's request. This permits the utility to sell gas at off-peak prices to the interruptible customer during normal or warm weather, utilizing the full capabilities of the pipeline system supplying gas to the area, while reserving an adequate supply of gas for the residential and commercial heating customers during periods of extremely cold weather. Gas turbines are flexible users of fuel and have reliable starting characteristics on many types of fuel. Dual fuel systems employing natural gas and fuel oil or LPG, which are capable of rapid changeover, are available from several turbine manufacturers and others are developing similar systems. Such systems enhance the value of turbine power to many customers and are valuable to many gas utilities for balancing pipeline demands.

Liquid Fuels

By far the greatest number of gas turbines in service today use liquid fuel. Liquid fuels are used exclusively to power gas turbines for aircraft service and with few exceptions, for marine and mobile ground use. As yet, except for aircraft specifications, there is no liquid fuel labeled "gas turbine fuel." Gas turbines have successfully used alcohol, gasoline, stove oil, diesel and heavy residual oil. This versatility of fuel use is an advantage which gas turbines have over reciprocating engines.

Fuel specifications have been established for military and civil aviation turbine fuels. The first turbojets used kerosene. JP-1 is primarily a kerosene type fuel and is still in use extensively by many foreign airlines. Perhaps the most common liquid fuel in service today for gas turbine use is JP-4. It is used for both military and civilian turbojets. JP-4 is a blend of light distillate oils ranging from gasoline to diesel oil. JP-5 is coming into popular use and is best described as a water-white diesel oil. JP-5 has an advantage over JP-4 and previous JP-series fuel in that it is less volatile. This reduces vapor losses and inflammability hazards for aircraft use. However, carbon forming tendencies are greater with JP-5. Turbines designed for the lighter fuels may require fuel system modification for the heavier fuel.

Large turbines used for stationary power have been designed to burn residual oil to reduce fuel cost. Experience is indicating that it is more economical to use a premium liquid fuel such as propane or butane because the elimination of processing charges for residual oils and lower turbine maintenance cost will offset the higher fuel cost. Prospective small turbine stationary installations relying on normal liquid fuel delivery service probably will use household furnace oil (No. 2 or furnace diesel) or diesel engine fuel.

Liquid fuels are easily stored. Relatively large reserves of fuel to operate gas turbines for many hours may be stored in tanks of various shapes at little or no positive pressure for aircraft and other mobile uses. Large reserves for stationary power use are easily provided. However, the provision of storage facilities is costly and may be avoided if natural gas is available on a firm service basis.

The light oil distillate fuels are easy to pump into the engine fuel system because they require much less volume than gaseous fuels for equal energy release. However, the heavy grades of liquid fuel create a greater maintenance problem because of the presence of sulfur and vanadium. This often results in undesirable deposits, erosion and corrosion in the hot portions of the turbine. The normal turbine design provides a stoichiometric mixture of fuel and air in the primary combustion zone in the combustors with the immediate introduction of secondary air to avoid combustor liner wall deterioration. This is accomplished more readily with lighter grade fuels. Natural gas is ideal for this purpose.

If the exhaust gases are to be used directly in an industrial process, natural gas provides a clean exhaust and is generally acceptable even for food processing. The exhaust gases become dirtier and less acceptable with liquid fuels, especially heavy oils.

Air pollution could become a problem in the employment of turbines using heavier grades of fuel oil, especially at idling speeds, but this is largely a function of burner design.

Solid Fuels

Solid fuels, such as coal, have been used experimentally as a turbine fuel but ash deposits limit the life of the turbine appreciably. However, considerable experimentation work is being conducted by the U. S. Bureau of Mines in this field. The equipment to utilize solid fuel adds greatly to the complexity and cost of the system, particularly when the energy release is indirect. Wood and peat have also been used as well as solid missile propellant. Nuclear fuel is a possibility for the future.

The solid fuel field is so specialized that it is considered beyond the scope of this book.

CHAPTER 4

System Components

Items of equipment necessary for operation but not included as a part of the turbine assembly are referred to as system components. The selection of these items is dependent on the engine application and the operating environment. Where a question exists regarding the suitability of equipment the turbine manufacturer should be consulted. In this chapter system components are considered as affecting the Intake Air System or the Turbine Shaft Load and are discussed under these headings.

Intake Air System

Gas turbine intake air systems require considerable design effort to meet the needs of the turbine. In detail these are as follows:

Air filtering
Air cooling
Sound attenuation
Anti-icing protection
Weather protection
Compressor cleaning

Intake systems generally consist of ductwork and plenum chambers that bring outdoor air directly to the turbine compressor inlet. The system may also contain one or more of the equipment items described later. Outdoor air is brought directly to the turbine because of the high air consumption rate of the gas turbine and the desirablity of keeping inlet air temperature at a low level. Inlet depression must also be kept as low as possible. A typical recommendation is 2 inches of water inlet depression at the engine rated power. Greater depression would require engine de-rating. Bends, where necessary, must be of large radius, and abrupt section changes should be avoided.

As a general design precaution, the intake system ductwork and components mounted inside must be securely assembled to prevent eventual loosening or breakage with subsequent ingestion by the turbine. Nuts and bolts located on the inner surface of ductwork should be regarded with suspicion where there is any possibility of loosening or fracture. Prior to the first start-up of a new gas turbine installation, the intake system should be thoroughly cleaned and inspected for loose items and other foreign matter.

Intake Air Filters

The necessity for filtering gas turbine intake air is not in some respects as acute as for filtering piston engine intake air. However, the final decision on an air filtering system requires a study of conditions at the installation site for possible unusual inlet air characteristics.

The following summarizes gas turbine foreign body ingestion hazards and means of preventing damage:

Type of Foreign Object	Engine Damage	Prevention
Small hard objects (gravel, hail)	Compressor blade nicking, bending, or fracture	Screen
Finely divided abrasives (sand and dust)	Compressor and turbine blade erosion	Dust filter
Large blanketing objects (birds, paper, rags)	Compressor blade jamming and fracture or air passage blockage	Filter, inspect and clean periodically
Insects	Compressor fouling	Filter, inspect and clean periodically
Solid Water	Flameout, possible compressor blade fracture	Anti-splash louvers
Oily vapor	Compressor fouling	Routine cleaning

The section of a gas turbine that sustains the greatest damage from foreign particle ingestion is the compressor. This is because the compressor is the first piece of equipment encountered by the foreign object. The resulting impingement force on contacting the moving parts of the compressor rotating at high speed can result in considerable damage.

Centrifugal compressors are less susceptible to damage than axial compressors because the centrifugal compressor impeller is more massive with relatively few blades of heavy section.

At installations where the turbine uses dust-laden air, more elaborate air filtering must be considered. Research has shown that air-borne dust, if sufficiently concentrated and of sufficient particle size, will cause destructive erosion of compressors and turbines. These research results can be summarized as follows:

(1) Dust particles 2–3 microns and smaller in diameter have little effect on turbine components other than polishing of the compressor;

(2) The larger the dust particles the more rapid is the erosion of turbine components; and

(3) Total turbine component erosion is a direct function of the total weight of ingested dust.

Air-borne dust survey research reported in the *ASHRAE Guide* shows outdoor air dust concentrations as measured in three cities:

Minneapolis	2.06×10^{-6} grams per cu ft
Pittsburgh	2.32×10^{-6} grams per cu ft
Louisville	3.42×10^{-6} grams per cu ft

Dust particle size distribution was found to be as follows:

99.99%	less than 25 microns
88%	less than 10 microns
65%	less than 5 microns
50%	less than 3 microns

As a general precaution against dust erosion, the turbine inlet should be located as far from dust generating sources as possible. Where air-borne dust can be present in any magnitude either on a continuous basis or from periodic dust storms an intake air filtering system is required.

The gas turbine is very sensitive to inlet pressure losses. The pressure drop through the intake filter must therefore be kept as low as possible.

Two general types of filter are applicable. These are (a) the extended area filter and (b) the inertial separator. The extended area filter is simply an array of filter panels of a suitable filter medium through which all of the intake air passes. A dry type of filter is preferable because of the possibility of carry-over from oil-wetted surfaces with subsequent compressor fouling. The filter medium should be capable of removing most of the dust larger than 2 to 3 microns. Clean filter pressure drop must be about one-half inch of water to allow an operating margin. Arrangements must be provided to monitor the pressure drop so that the filter can be cleaned or replaced when necessary. The extended area filter has the advantages of low cost and simplicity but it is bulky and requires periodic servicing.

The inertial separator utilizes the greater mass of the entrained dust particles to separate them from the air stream. In operation, the separator forces the air stream to change direction. The dust particles, unable to change direction as readily as the air, follow a different path than the air and are thus removed. Two effective inertial separators are the dust louver type and the cyclone type. Both types use scavenging air to remove the dust that has separated from the inlet air. A scavenging blower, usually electric motor-driven, is required with an air flow of 10% of the inlet flow. Inertial filters are thus self-cleaning, but there must be storage and clean-out provisions at the ultimate dust collection point. Pressure drop does not increase with use. Inertial separators have the advantage of small size and are self-cleaning but require the scavenging air system and will probably be more expensive installed than extended area filters.

As a general rule, then, as to filter choice in dusty locations, the extended area filter should be used.

Intake Air Cooling

The gas turbine output rating is based on a certain mass air flow rate through the machine. The compressor, which is a constant volume device, is sized to handle the correct volume of air at the rating temperature, usually 60 or 80 deg F. If the intake air temperature rises, the mass flow of air through the turbine must decrease in accordance with the gas laws. For instance, an engine handling an air flow of 20 lb per sec at 80 deg F will handle an air flow of 19.28 lb per sec at 100 deg F. The 3.5% reduction in air mass flow will show up as reduced output power. The compressor is also hampered by a decrease in pressure ratio when intake air temperature rises, thus compounding the output power loss. Furthermore, the engine's thermal efficiency is a function of the ratio of burner outlet temperature to engine intake temperature. An intake temperature rise thus has a detrimental effect on fuel consumption as well as on power output.

Cooling of the intake air during periods of high ambient temperature is therefore beneficial. Cooling can be done by mechanical refrigeration or simply by water evaporation. Where cooling is employed, the selection of method should be on an economic basis.

A water evaporation cooler consists of a set of extended area air filters, and an array of nozzles to spray water onto the filter upstream surface. When the intake air passes over the wet surfaces its temperature will be reduced as it evaporates water. A secondary benefit will be the addition to the mass flow through the turbine by the amount of water vapor taken up by the intake air. The cooler should be placed as close as possible to the entrance of the intake air ducting system so that the system handles cooled air and so that the maximum time for vaporization of entrained water is available. Where an intake air filter is used, the cooler should be placed immediately downstream of the filter. Some precautions are needed to prevent water carry-over into the compressor. Air velocity through the cooler panels should be kept below 250 ft per min to avoid droplet entrainment. Cooling of the air too close to the wet bulb or saturation temperature of the ambient air should not be attempted (not less than 10 deg F margin is a safe value) to preclude the possibility of subsequent water drop-out and accumulation on the duct walls. Such accumulated water may eventually separate from the duct and enter the compressor as a damaging slug.

Centrifugal compressor turbines have been operated with a water cooling system consisting only of a spray nozzle spraying directly into the compressor inlet. A water flow rate equal to the fuel flow rate is practical. The chief disadvantage of this simple system is that any dissolved solids in the water will deposit on the compressor blades on evaporation of the water and this eventually will adversely affect engine performance.

Anti-Icing Equipment

Under the atmospheric condition in which the air contains supercooled water, gas turbine inlet icing can occur. Ice will build up when the air impinging on metal surfaces is below 40 deg F. When an ice layer builds up on the turbine inlet fairing the air flow area decreases, thus choking the engine and causing the turbine inlet temperature to rise. Another hazard is that accumulated ice may break off in large chunks and pass through the engine, damaging the compressor.

Ice can easily be prevented from forming by supplying heat to the inlet system components against which the air stream impinges. Usually electrical resistance heating elements are the most convenient means of supplying heat. Control of the anti-icing system can be keyed to an ice detector or, more simply, to inlet air temperature. In the latter case, the anti-ice heat should be turned on when engine inlet temperature falls to 40 deg F.

Intake Sound Attenuation

One of the more noticeable characteristics of a running gas turbine is the loud high frequency sound that emanates from the compressor inlet. The sound is very offensive to the human ear and in most installations must be eliminated. Fortunately, high frequency sound is strongly directional and can be readily absorbed. Intake sound attenuation systems take advantage of these characteristics. The system should eliminate any straight line path from the sound source (compressor inlet) to the observer's ear. If the intake ducting already contains one or more bends, this requirement is satisfied. If the intake is a straight-through duct, then baffles in the duct and off the duct mouth will be required. The duct walls and all the baffle surfaces that "see" the compressor should be lined with a sound absorbing material. The material should be attached to duct surfaces by suitable mechanical fasteners in addition to an adhesive to prevent loosening and subsequent ingestion of the material by the compressor. Detailed recommendations for sound absorbing materials and techniques should be obtained from the engine manufacturer.

Weather Louvers

As an item of general good practice, the intake duct opening should be protected by weather louvers. The louvers will protect against solid water impingement and freezing rain.

Compressor Cleaning

Long-time operation of a gas turbine will result in a gradual build-up of an oily deposit on the compressor components. The deposit is black in color and slightly sticky to the touch. It clings tenaciously to the surfaces on which it is deposited. It appears that this deposit is merely normal pollution present in metropolitan atmospheres that precipitates on the compressor. Engine performance will gradually deteriorate as the deposit builds up. This deterioration will be detectable as an increase in exhaust gas temperature over that of the new engine exhaust temperature for a given load. When the exhaust temperature has risen to the engine manufacturer's condemning limit, compressor cleaning will restore the temperature to the new engine range.

Compressor cleaning methods recommended by the engine manufacturer should be followed. An accepted method consists of feeding an approved cleaning abrasive such as ground walnut shells into the compressor inlet of a running engine. The air inlet duct or plenum should contain access panels immediately adjacent to the compressor inlet to permit introduction of the cleaning compound and inspection of the compressor. In any case, the engine manufacturer should be consulted to obtain specific recommendations for his particular engine.

Fuel Compressor

The gas turbine requires natural gas supplied to the burner system at a pressure higher than the air pressure within the combustor. The actual fuel pressure required depends on the engine burner and fuel system design. Fuel supply pressure requirements will therefore vary considerably among engine manufacturers. Currently, pressures range between 60 and 240 psig. Where adequate gas line pressure for the turbine needs is not available, a gas fuel compressor must be provided.

Natural gas compressors are commercially available from manufacturers of air compressors. There are two general types: rotary vaned compressors and reciprocating piston compressors. Choosing the compressor for a particular installation requires close coordination with the engine and compressor manufacturer. If the engine manufacturer provides a drive for a compressor, his recommendations must be followed. Where an engine drive is not provided, the compressor must be driven by an auxiliary source. The fuel compressor will require some form of jacket cooling and, if staged, for interstage cooling. Cooling may be by water or air.

When the fuel compressor is direct-driven by the gas turbine, or is driven by electric power produced by the turbine, a supply of pressurized gas is needed for engine start-up. The method of providing start-up fuel will depend on its frequency of usage. Some possible methods are: Bottled LPG; auxiliary start-up fuel compressor driven by an electric motor from batteries; auxiliary start-up fuel compressor driven by the gas turbine's cranking energy source; main compressor driven by an auxiliary electric motor, battery-powered, and main compressor driven by the gas turbine's cranking energy source.

A control system will be required to shift from the start-up fuel source to the regular fuel system when the turbine becomes self-sustaining.

External Lubrication System

A gas turbine installation will require some form of engine oil cooler. The turbine manufacturer will provide information regarding the lubrication oil heat rejection rate, oil flow rate, engine oil-out temperature, and required engine oil-in temperature. These data will make possible the selection of a suitable oil cooler from normal sources. Usually a supply of water is available permitting the use of a water-to-oil cooler. If cooling water is not available, an air-to-oil cooler can be used. Cooling air movement through the oil cooler is generally best provided by an electric motor-driven fan.

Some gas turbines also require an external motor-driven lubrication pump and related piping to permit circulation of lubricating oil prior to engine start-up and during engine coastdown. This auxiliary lubrication system must be integrated into the regular lubricating system according to the engine maker's instructions.

Output Gearbox

An inherent characteristic of the gas turbine is high rotational speed. This will range from about 10,000 rpm for large machines to 40,000 rpm or more for small engines. The engine manufacturer furnishes reduction gearing as an integral part of his engine to provide useable output shaft speeds. The gears in the output gearbox are of precision high speed type. The gear and bearing lubrication system is a part of the general engine lubrication system. Since speed matching of the turbine wheel to its load is important, most turbine manufacturers offer a variety of output reduction gear ratios. The manufacturer may also provide ratios outside his standard offerings on special order.

Exhaust Heat Recovery Equipment

One of the characteristics of the gas turbine is the very large quantity of heat available in the exhaust gas. The economics of most gas turbine installations dictate that this heat be utilized. The use to which the exhaust heat is put (heating water, making steam, heating air, and so on) is determined by the type of installation. The following remarks, however, apply generally to all exhaust heat devices.

The gas turbine is sensitive to exhaust back pressure. The specification for any exhaust gas heat exchanger must therefore specify the hot gas side allowable pressure drop. A target value for this pressure drop is between 3 and 5 inches of water. Where additional heat is supplied to the boiler by direct firing it may be necessary to operate with a higher pressure drop. Recommendations of the turbine manufacturer will determine the upper pressure limit.

Gas turbine exhaust while burning natural gas is probably the cleanest of any internal combustion engine. Combustion efficiencies are of the order of 98% and there is no contamination from lubricating oil. Therefore the exhaust heat recovery equipment needs no provision for hot side cleaning.

The exhaust gas temperature and flow depend on the engine model and the load at which it is operating. This information is available in the form of curves from the engine manufacturer. As a general approximation, rated load exhaust temperature may be taken as 1000 deg F and rated load exhaust flow as 10 to 15 standard cfm per horsepower.

Use of exhaust heat recovery equipment requires a control system to regulate the quantity of heat delivered by the heat exchanger. A common method involves the use of an exhaust duct by-passing the heat exchanger to permit partial use of the engine exhaust flow when heat demand is low (the exhaust bypass system is discussed below in the next paragraph). An alternative heat control system is one that passes all of the engine exhaust through the heat exchanger and regulates the flow of the cold medium through the heat exchanger. A waste heat boiler with this type of control system is in common use having the boiler water level regulated in accordance with the heat demand.

Outlet Bypass and Dampers

Exhaust waste heat recovery systems must provide for variation in heat supply. One means for providing this is an exhaust bypass duct with an adequate damper for flow regulation. Engine exhaust thus has two parallel routes to atmosphere; one path goes through the heat recovery device, the other path directly to the atmosphere through the bypass duct. The amount of hot gas delivered to the heat recovery device is regulated by a damper valve installed in the bypass duct. A control system is employed to modulate the bypass damper valve in accordance with the temperature of the heated product.

Outlet Sound Attenuator

Attenuation of gas turbine exhaust noise must be provided at installation sites to satisfy noise restriction requirements. The exhaust noise is of low frequency, around 300 cycles per second, and can be described as a steady roar. Exhaust heat recovery equipment functions very well as an exhaust noise attenuator. Ordinarily the installation of heat recovery equipment, such as waste heat boilers or exhaust gas-to-air heat exchangers, will take care of the exhaust noise problem.

Where heat recovery equipment is not installed exhaust noise attenuation can be accomplished by suitable exhaust mufflers or by baffled exhaust ducts employing sound absorption techniques satisfying local fire protection requirements.

CHAPTER 5

Installation Requirements

Installation requirements for industrial gas turbine engines are as many and varied as the number of applications. Each installation has certain features which will undoubtedly be peculiar to that installation or at least to that type of installation. The fundamental requirements common to all industrial gas turbine installations are dealt with in this chapter.

Machine Mount

Generally, industrial gas turbines are supplied by the manufacturer complete with an integral base which supports the basic engine and the various accessories required for the particular installation, such as starting motor, accessories gearbox, engine driven fuel and lubrication pumps, auxiliary fuel and lubrication pumps, and a reduction gearbox if required. In some instances the base may be extended to support the driven component (pumps, generator, etc.). The base should be designed to preclude pockets of inflammable fuel or lubricating oil vapor. The consulting engineer or architect-engineer must follow this up by insuring that the actual installation site is adequately safeguarded against similar hazards. If engines are to be installed in a foundation pit of any kind, forced ventilation of the pit should be provided.

Foundations

One of the advantages of the industrial gas turbine is the virtually vibration-free operation of the unit. From an installation standpoint this results in two distinct advantages: (a) there is no need to provide isolation between the machine mount and the foundation to prevent the transfer of vibration (although some manufacturers do recommend isolation pads, or mounts in some installations), and (b) massive foundations capable of withstanding reciprocating loads are unnecessary. Gas turbines lend themselves particularly to roof installation.

Depending on the weight of the equipment, the inertia of rotating parts (WR^2), and the characteristics of the connected equipment (including the braking characteristics of the generator under short circuit conditions, where it forms the main load) a load of 1.2 times the dead weight of the equipment may suffice in design of the foundations.

Inlet and Exhaust Ducting

The inlet and exhaust ducting used in the installation of an industrial gas turbine are largely dependent on the special requirements of the application.

Inlet ducting will be required to mate with intake filter, cooler or silencer, as needed, and with the engine intake. While thermal expansion problems in the intake system are not severe, an expansion joint should be provided at the engine intake and perhaps elsewhere, depending on the length and complexity of the system. Expansion bellows of the rubberized fabric type will usually be adequate.

Since a 1% loss in intake pressure will result in approximately 2½% loss in engine power, careful design of the intake system is important, particularly where duct velocities are over, say, 100 feet per second, and dynamic head is a significant fraction of total pressure. Where a 90° change in direction of the air stream is required, vaned corners will provide minimum loss, approximately 13% of the dynamic head. An elbow in which the bend radius of the center line is 3 times the diameter of the duct or pipe (i. e. 3D elbow) will give a loss of about 15% of dynamic head, and a 2D elbow, 20%.

Sudden increases in duct cross-section in total area, or in either longitudinal plane, should be avoided. If it is necessary to discharge air from a relatively low velocity volume such as the plenum behind an intake filter, a bell mouth entry to the duct will give minimum loss. A convergent section of 30° included angle may also be used or a convergent section of 90° included angle with a fairing of generous radius at the entrance to the duct.

Exhaust ducting may lead directly to the stack, as illustrated in Figs. 5–1 and 5–2, or through a recuperative heat exchanger as in

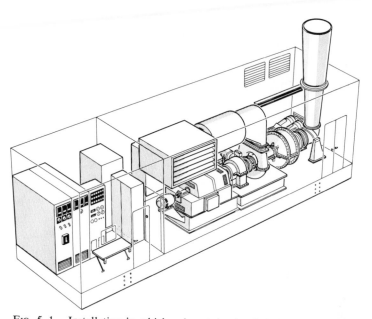

FIG. 5–1.   Installation in which exhaust ducting is led directly to stack

Fig. 5–3.   It may also lead to a waste heat boiler, silencer, or other unit, or combination of units before entering the stack.   Further requirements for exhaust duct installation are given in National Fire Protection Association Bulletin 37.

Up to a gas temperature of approximately 900 deg F, mild steel exhaust ducting will be adequate for most installations.   Above this temperature, specialized low alloy steels should be considered to minimize corrosion.   Expansion joints in exhaust ducting must accommodate considerable thermal expansion in the ducting and in the hot end of the engine, and are highly stressed.   These should be fabricated from an appropriate stainless steel.   When they are located in a high velocity section of the exhaust ducting, or when the engine will burn a fuel which could produce deposits interfering with free

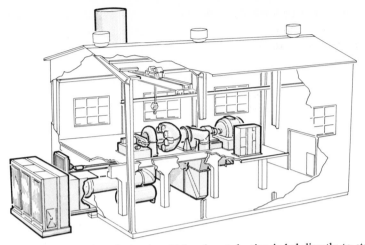

Fig. 5-2.   Another installation in which exhaust ducting is led directly to stack

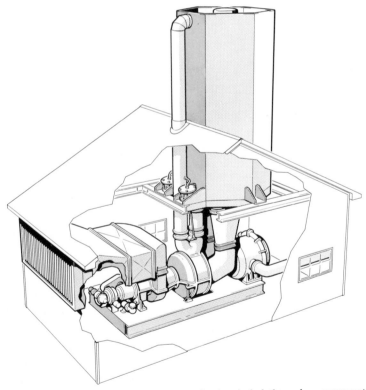

Fig. 5-3.   Installation in which exhaust ducting is led through a recuperative
heat exchanger

flexing of the bellows, the joints may be fitted with an inner sleeve. Where the ducting is insulated, the expansion joint should also be fitted with an outer sleeve.

The foregoing comments on the aerodynamic design of intake ducting are generally applicable to exhaust ducting. A 1% reduction in turbine back pressure will cause an increase in available power of about 1½%, and the ducting and stack must be designed gradually to reduce the gas velocity for maximum recovery of dynamic head.

Losses in the intake and exhaust ducting have less effect on the performance of gas turbines with high compression ratios. The best result is provided by a conical diffuser of, for usual lengths, about 7° included angle. Greater or smaller angles will give an increase in pressure loss. For practical reasons, rectangular diffusers are often preferred, and when two walls of a rectangular diffuser are parallel, the diverging walls should have an angle between 8° and 10°. When all walls of a rectangular diffuser are diverging, an included angle of 6° is appropriate. Where space limitations dictate, a rectangular diffuser of higher outside angle may be provided with a system of splitters to provide a number of passages, each one of which has the optimum internal angles.

Some engines require external piping for carrying compressor delivery air to the high pressure side of a recuperative heat exchanger, and for carrying the heated air back to the engine combustion system inlet. This ducting is generally commercial steel pipe of a gauge appropriate to the pressure and temperatures. Bends should preferably be long radius, and duct lengths kept as short as possible. See Fig. 5–3.

Bellows expansion joints are a special problem, due to the pneumatic ram effect of the air at compressor delivery pressure. There must be special restraint to prevent "flip out" of a section of pipe between two bellows, and to eliminate the very substantial loads on the engine and recuperator casings. Where engine and recuperator flanges have intersecting center lines and permit an arc-shaped piping layout, a three joint layout using hinge-pinned expansion bellows resolves pneumatic and dynamic loads to a hoop tension of low value, and permits relative motion of the engine and recuperator flanges in the plane of the pipe centerline.

In some installations, accessibility to the engine itself is improved by arranging the ductwork to enter and leave the engine from below, as in Fig. 5–2, and this is important with large sizes where heavy lifting equipment is required for removal of casings for inspection.

Ductwork in these cases should be particularly well designed for long life to avoid replacement.

Fuel System

Vibration isolation of fuel supply lines to a gas turbine is not generally a problem, however, the installation should conform to local codes and NFPA regulations.

The diameter of the lines will depend on the type of fuel being carried, the permissible pressure losses in the lines, and their lengths. The tables in Appendix C of the proposed ASA Z83.1, "American Standard for Installation of Gas Piping and Gas Equipment on Industrial Premises and Other Premises," will be useful in determining sizes of gas piping.

The proposed ASA Z83.1 provides much useful information on the installation of gas piping and gas equipment on industrial and other premises. It is recommended that it be read in conjunction with this book.

Gas suppliers' meters are normally installed by the gas company. An outside area, or a suitably ventilated indoor space should be allocated, in consultation with the gas company for the installation of their meters.

Consumer owned gas meters should be installed in accordance with Section 5.1 of the proposed ASA Z83.1 referred to above.

As a convenience for periodic engine performance checks on the gas turbine, a meter of the pressure differential type may be installed on the gas supply line to each engine. If it is desired to check liquid fuel performance on a dual fuel engine, the liquid fuel meter installed will normally be of the rotometer or turbine type.

Natural gas is often available only at low pressure and must be compressed for use in a gas turbine. As it is impractical to introduce fuel with the air at the inlet to the engine, a separate pump, or pumps, must be installed to deliver gas at a pressure with sufficient margin over engine compressor delivery to provide for operating control.

This compressor is not normally included in the engine assembly. It may be electric motor driven or driven from the gas turbine shaft. The compressor will absorb 5 to 10% of the gas turbine output depending on the available gas pressure and the engine pressure ratio. Gas turbines supplied with high pressure gas avoid these losses.

At locations where power for running a gas compressor is in short supply, or if a turbine shaft driven compressor is used, it may be desirable to start the gas turbine on liquid fuel. Once it is running and producing power to run the compressor, the gas turbine can then be switched over to run on the compressed gas. Not all gas turbines permit change-over during running.

Instrumentation

The amount of instrumentation associated with a gas turbine can vary considerably but would ordinarily include indications of the following variables:

> Rpm of power turbine
> Rpm of gas producer, if separate
> Exhaust temperature
> Lubricating oil pressure
> Fuel supply pressure
> Oil cooler temperature, in
> Oil cooler temperatures, out
> Oil tank level

Other items which might be instrumented would be:

> Air inlet depression
> Oil filter differential pressure
> Fuel filter differential pressure
> Fuel tank quantity indicator
> Fuel flow meter
> Scavenge oil temperature
> Flame out detection
> Engine vibration
> Fuel flow rate
> Special instrumentation related to engine design

As a matter of convenience, some data from the driven equipment, such as generator current, voltage, KVA, and frequency, may appear on the engine control panel.

The most important items, such as output rpm and exhaust temperature, may be continuously recorded or may be read on a regular schedule along with other significant indications and recorded manually for future reference.

Many of the indications do not need to be shown numerically, since it matters only if certain limits are exceeded. Warning light and/or audible alarms are adequate in these cases. Automatic control devices to prevent damage to equipment are usually incorporated to provide shut-down of the gas turbine under conditions of excessive speed, excessive exhaust temperature or lack of oil pressure.

On dual fuel engines, change-over from one fuel to another may be automatic when the supply of one fuel is interrupted.

Certain instruments may require electrical power for their operation and, in addition, continuous operation of the gas turbine may depend on a continuous supply of electrical power. This may be DC with a battery bank and charger, or AC, with some means of maintaining it in the event of failure of the main power source. Even engines with completely pneumatic control systems require electrical power for the ignition circuit during engine start.

Lubrication System

The lubrication of a gas turbine is normally provided by a gearbox driven pump supplied with oil from a tank built into the base of the engine. For starting and for cooling on shut down, as well as for emergency use, an auxiliary pump powered by some other source such as batteries or gas expansion motors may be required. The system would include a pressure regulating valve, liquid level gauge, filter (s), and associated valves, but the cooler is often separate from the engine.

An oil-to-water cooler is most economical in first cost and is recommended in locations where a reliable source of low cost water is available. Control will normally be by a thermostatically operated bypass at the inlet to the cooler.

Oil to air coolers are more expensive than the oil-to-water type, particularly if high ambient air temperatures are to be accommodated. If their size and cost becomes excessive, consideration should be given to the use of a high-temperature oil. The temperature can be controlled in many ways, including variable fan speed and modulating dampers, both of which are superior to by-passing the oil around the cooler since they save fan power.

Water System

Water is not required for the operation of a gas turbine alone, but it is often needed by equipment associated with one, such as evaporative air inlet cooler, lubricating oil cooler, gas compressor intercooler, or waste heat boiler. The boiler will require its own feedwater pumps but the remaining equipment can be supplied from the mains. Piping should conform to A.S.A. B31.1.

Sound Attenuation

Sound generated by a gas turbine is largely in the intake and exhaust and, in many installations, acoustical treatment of the gas turbine enclosure or power plant walls will be required to attenuate sound generated by the accessories. See previous chapter.

A commercial intake silencer of the acoustic splitter vane or cylindrical type will usually be required. It should be specified on the basis of allowable pressure drop, normally from ½ to 1 inch of water, at design point air weight flow, and on the basis of desired sound attenuation. A typical silencer has an attenuation of 16 decibels in the third octave band (75 to 150 cps), increasing to 40 decibels in the sixth octave band (1200 to 2400 cps). Higher attenuations can be achieved by increasing passage length, and to maintain the same pressure drop, by increasing flow area.

If the intake system has a right-angled bend, acoustic treatment of the duct walls may provide sufficient attenuation, but the acoustic performance of such an arrangement is difficult to predict with any degree of certainty, and special care will be required to ensure that bits of acoustic material and miscellaneous items of hardware will not work loose and be drawn through the engine.

The intake filter and intake cooler (if used) do not provide significant attenuation.

Exhaust silencers are also commercially available. They may be of the de-tuner type, or generally similar to intake silencers in configuration. Due to the high low frequency content of the sound, and due to the elevated temperatures, exhaust silencers are comparatively expensive. When a recuperative heat exchanger is installed as in Fig. 5-3, it is rarely necessary to install an outlet silencer. Many boiler designs provide moderate silencing, and a separate silencer may be eliminated or reduced in size. In non-critical locations a carefully designed simple stack arrangement, as in Figs. 5-1 and 5-2, may provide adequate silencing, since jet shear, the principal component of noise from a high-velocity exhaust system, varies as the eighth power of jet velocity, and will be insignificant if the exhaust system provides controlled diffusion down to exhaust velocities of, say, 50 feet per second.

Thermal Insulation

Thermal insulation of turbine and combustion system casings, exhaust ducts, heat exchanger ducting, and boilers is required for personnel protection and avoidance of excessive heat release to the building. Except for breeching connections to the stack, it reduces system losses and increases operating efficiency. Thermal insulation is also effective in reducing sound transmission. Special consideration should be given to the insulation of engine casings so that component removal for inspection is not made difficult. In low velocity sections of exhaust ducting, thermal insulation may be installed in the inside rather than the outside of the duct to provide absorption of high frequency noises which would otherwise be radiated up the stack.

Inside heated buildings, insulation of the intake system will avoid condensation and frost formation.

Ventilation

Ventilation in a gas turbine power plant will be required to remove heat radiated from the equipment and ducting. This may require as high as 10 air changes per hour. Hot surfaces within the building will normally be insulated to provide a skin temperature of 150 deg F or less, and heat release can be calculated using standard formulas. Heat release from a gas turbine with short duct lengths may be as little as 3 Btu per hp hr. Heat release from a gas turbine and connected waste heat boiler or recuperator located within the building may be 300 Btu per hp hr., and appropriate air change capacity will be required. Consideration must also be given to the connected load. A generator has a full load efficiency of about 96 percent and the remaining 4 percent of energy input is converted to heat. If the generator is "self cooled" from building air, the heat release adds an additional 100 Btu per hp hr., to the heat load.

Internal ventilation of the gas turbine is handled automatically by the engine itself during regular operation. The gaseous fuel and lubricating oil vapor which may be present inside the engine at rest should be purged by motoring the engine prior to ignition and the introduction of fresh fuel. When equipment such as a waste heat boiler is installed in the exhaust from the turbine, it may be advantageous to use a separate blower to reduce the purging time and save energy, since the gas turbine is not particularly effective as a fan at normal motoring speeds.

Accessibility

Space should be provided for access to a gas turbine for maintenance. This should include clearance for removal of parts as they are withdrawn, and a place to put them while further work is being done. This problem will be made more difficult by overhead ductwork and piping and will be simplified by adequate lifting facilities.

While a moderately large opening may be required to pass a gas turbine to its mounting position, it should never be necessary to replace the whole unit in service. Permanent passages and doorways need be only large enough to accommodate the largest individual part. In the case of gas turbine driven electrical generator sets (Figs. 5–1 and 5–2), the parts of the generator are likely to be larger and heavier than those of the gas turbine.

Electrical Services

Electrical services to a gas turbine are always required for ignition, and usually for instrumentation, control, and starting as well. The supply may come from a public utility, batteries, an independent auxiliary generator, a gas turbine driven generator and more often, a combination of these. The choice depends on many factors involving cost and reliability.

Operational Control

Gas turbine plants are well suited to automatic and semiautomatic operation and, consequently, can be operated by relatively inexperienced personnel. An annunciator panel will generally be provided, which will indicate the source of potential trouble or the reason for a shut-down. Once the difficulty is corrected, the same panel will indicate that the gas turbine is ready for restart. The actual starting operation will often consist of selecting the appropriate fuel and pushing a start button, and then, once the engine is self sustaining, setting the required speed. In the case of electric generator drives, the generators can then be synchronized, if necessary, and loaded.

In the case of a multi-unit gas turbine generator installation, it will be advantageous to install automatic load sensing equipment for adding additional sets as required to maintain optimum loading. Such a system should have provision for interchanging the lead or master unit so that the set which is one week "first on, last off," may the next week be "last on, first off" to equalize wear on the various sets.

Instrumentation of the equipment in a gas turbine plant should be arranged so that indications of difficulties are brought to the attention of the operator at one point, probably in an office adjacent to the machinery room. The control equipment may also be centralized, or may be located close to units which it controls. Certain operations such as speed setting may be controlled from both a local engine control panel and an electrical control center.

The local codes and ordinances and regulations governing the installation of gas turbines and their associated equipment should be investigated and complied with, by the person or agency making or authorizing the installation.

CHAPTER 6

Applications

Gas turbine engines can be designed to give a variety of different performance characteristics. In this chapter some of these differences are described and examples are given to illustrate how they can be applied to advantage in various applications. Although all of the possible applications for gas turbines cannot be described or foreseen, it is hoped that the examples given here will illustrate certain basic principles which can be applied, to determine how a gas turbine may be used to advantage in a new application.

Following is an illustration of several typical gas turbine characteristics together with the application where that feature is best applied:

Characteristics	Applications
Low weight and small size	Highway common carrier to obtain increased payload. Military vehicle to obtain low silhouette.
Quick starting	Stand-by power for emergency or peaking operation to replace spinning reserves.
Automatic control	Remotely located unmanned pumping stations.
Ease of using waste heat (with or without reheat)	Drying kilns, furnaces and steam boilers for heat or refrigeration in a Total Energy System.

Application Principles

The selection of the proper prime mover configuration for a given application is extremely important. Several of the important factors regarding turbine selection are discussed briefly in the following paragraphs. There are many more-complex cycle arrangements which could be considered, however, they are of more interest to the turbine designer and are not discussed here.

Industrial Gas Turbine or a Modified Aircraft Type Engine. Generally speaking, the industrial turbine is used in continuous duty applications where the power requirements are large, long endurance life is needed, and there are no size restrictions. The compact type will generally be used in intermittent to moderately continuous applications where the power requirement is not greater than 10,000 to 12,000 horsepower and there are certain size and/or weight limitations. An installed initial cost versus maintenance cost trade-off study will greatly influence the selection for a particular application.

Single Shaft Turbine Versus a Free Turbine. There are certain applications where each type has an advantage. The free turbine is generally used in an application requiring wide speed variations. The automobile and truck are examples of this type of power requirement.

The single shaft turbine is generally used where the speed does not vary significantly or where accurate speed control with sudden load changes is required. An independent, base load electrical power generator has a requirement of this type.

Relationship of Prime Mover Shaft Power and Heat Outputs. The gas turbine as opposed to the reciprocating type engine is very adaptable to the recovery of what is sometimes referred to as by-product or "exhaust" heat. In a simple cycle reciprocating engine a portion of heat is discharged as energy in the exhaust gases. The remainder is discharged from the cooling radiator at a low temperature level. The gas turbine cycle discharges all its "exhaust" heat energy in the exhaust gases at a high temperature level thus permitting efficient and economical heat recovery.

The gas turbine exhaust gas also contains approximately 17% oxygen which could be used to support reheat combustion. Thus, a turbine incorporating a reheat burner could be used in a duty cycle which has a simultaneous requirement for low shaft power and high heat energy. In some cases this exhaust heat may be used directly in a furnace or drying kiln. It could be used to fire a steam boiler or as a heat source for an absorption refrigeration unit. Likewise, a steam or refrigerant boiler may be used to drive a turbine for additional shaft power in a closed cycle system.

Thermal efficiencies for simple cycle turbines currently available will normally range from 12 to 24%. The turbine-boiler combinations will run from 77 to 82%. (Efficiencies are based on the higher heating value of natural gas.)

Typical Applications

The following examples illustrate some common gas turbine advantages and applications as prime movers.

Highway Common Carrier. The gross weight of highway transportation vehicles is limited by legislation. Therefore, vehicle payload can be significantly increased by using a lightweight, compact gas turbine unit. In addition, a free turbine engine would simplify the transmission as the power turbine would function as a torque converter, thus reducing the number of gear shifts required. By employing a regenerative cycle in the gas turbine, fuel economies approaching a diesel or gasoline reciprocating engine are realized.

Locomotives. Railroads that make long and heavy runs over rough mountainous terrain have been the largest users of gas turbine locomotives. The high horsepower-low speed requirement for this type of job are ideally suited to a free turbine engine. This type locomotive must also have dimensions that are within railroad clearance limitations. Therefore, if a reciprocating type engine is used, cooling radiator size becomes a power limiting factor. These features, plus high load factors, have made the gas turbine attractive in this application.

Additional research is needed, however, to make the turbine more widely accepted for all locomotive applications.

Electric Power Generation. The public utility and industrial areas must be considered in the field of power generation as each will have different requirements. One very important consideration is whether the new unit is to be a separate electrical system or will be associated with a larger existing system. The separate system must maintain its own frequency control whereas the latter unit will have the frequency controlled by the main line. The major requirement for the latter unit is that it be brought into phase before "tie-in" with the main line, and be capable of carrying its share of the load.

In the utility area, a unit can be used for base load or peaking loads. These units can be remotely located because of their ability to be controlled automatically from distant main stations. This feature allows the units to be placed near the load to reduce transmission losses. A recent installation has demonstrated that gas turbines can replace steam spinning reserve units. This is due to the rapid starting and acceleration characteristic of the turbine-engine which allows full power output to be reached in less than two minutes. A significant advantage of gas turbine driven generators in power generation is the easy adaptability to a large steam-electric plant which is becoming obsolete or is near peak capacity. Relatively large "packages" of power can be added with small initial cost thus forestalling large capital investment until economically feasible. At the same time, turbine exhaust provides a means of increasing conventional steam cycle efficiency by as much as 5 to 10 percent by supplying preheated combustion air or heating feed water. When the final power installation is made, these "package" units can be moved to end-of-line peak loading or other stand-by service.

Gas Compression and Processing. The gas turbine is well suited to this application because the centrifugal gas compressors used in pumping stations have speed ranges which closely match those of the turbine engine. Therefore, a direct connection can be utilized which will eliminate unnecessary gearing.

Gas turbines are also used in the gas processing industry. These units are used to power the equipment required in the liquefaction of natural gas. The exhaust heat energy can be used to run additional pumping and refrigerating units.

Additional Applications

Additional applications of the gas turbine engine are listed and briefly discussed in order to illustrate the wide variety of uses that have been found for this type of power source.

Air Separation. In air separation plants, gas turbines drive centrifugal or axial compressors which supply large quantities of air for the separation cycle. In addition, exhaust heat is used for steam generation to drive generators, compressors and refrigeration in the processes.

Brick Industry. The Burns Brick Company was the first member of this industry to operate a turbine-generator unit. This unit, Fig.

6–1, supplies all the plant electric service for their conveyors, forming machines and driers.

Building and Plant Services. The Park Plaza Shopping Center in Little Rock, Arkansas was the first installation of this type. A gas turbine generator provides the shopping center electricity and the turbine exhaust energy is used to generate low pressure steam for heating and for air conditioning.

In the area of office building services, the Northern Illinois Gas Company has built two office buildings, both with the electric power

FIG. 6–1. Ruston-Hornsby gas turbine-generator which supplies all of the Burns Brick Company plant's electrical needs. Exhaust heat is used directly in plant's brick production process

and heating and cooling energy supplied by gas turbines. These are illustrated in Figs. 6–2 and 6–3. A unique part of these installations is the use of high frequency 420 cycle lighting. The high frequency lighting gives less heat load, longer lamp life, greater light level from fewer fixtures, and a whiter "no flicker" light. The larger of these two buildings is also the first completely automatic, multi-module installation. Four gas turbine generator sets employing unique "dual-frequency" alternators (60 cycle and 420 cycle output) are automatically controlled to come on or off as the building load requirement varies throughout the day, thus permitting a running turbine to operate at or near full load where it is most efficient.

Another example of a gas turbine-power generator office building services installation is one at the Southern California Gas Company

FIG. 6–2. Two AiResearch gas turbines, fueled by natural gas, which are the nucleus of the total energy system supplying all energy requirements at the Northern Illinois Gas Company's Glen Ellyn office building

office building in Downey, California. This setup employing the two turbine power centers pictured in Fig. 6–4 supplies all the electricity, heat and air conditioning for a 31,000 square foot building.

The first school building to use this Total Energy concept is located

FIG. 6-3. Thompson Ramo Wooldridge system employing a Continental gas turbine that supplies power and heat requirements for the Northern Illinois Gas Power Company's general office building in Aurora, Illinois

FIG. 6-4. These two Boeing Turbo-Power Centers supply all the electricity, heat and air conditioning for Southern California Gas Company's 31,000-square foot office building in Downey, California

in McAllen, Texas. With all electrical, heating and cooling and hot water services being provided by gas turbines, the school building would serve as an independent, self-sustaining community center in time of a disaster. The installation is shown in Fig. 6–5.

Chemical Industry. In chemical industry applications, the gas turbine provides compressor and electrical power as well as process steam. The turbine engine also provides hot gases for regeneration or reforming.

FIG. 6–5. Installation incorporating a Solar gas turbine (in cabinet) driving low and high frequency generators which supplies power, heat and cooling requirements for McAllen High School, McAllen, Texas

Food Processing. The natural gas-fired turbine exhaust is clean enough for use in food processing and is used for shaft power, generating units, and to provide exhaust energy for process steam.

Petroleum and Petrochemical. The Houdry process, which requires large quantities of hot gases, employs the gas generator portion of the turbine cycle. Through this process, end products are being produced economically by fully utilizing the gas turbine cycle.

Primary Metals. In the steel industry the drive for cost reduction has opened new avenues for the gas turbines. Unattended generating units can supply heavy electrical loads while the exhaust gas may be used for power or heat.

Military-National Defense. Gas turbines, using natural gas as a fuel provide all electric and heating requirements for Royal Canadian Air Force Pine Tree radar warning line stations. One such installation shown in Fig. 6–6 employs a 1600-horsepower turbine which drives a generator to produce up to 1100 kilowatts. The turbine exhaust, at 900 deg F, is ducted to an exhaust heat recovery boiler producing steam for heating.

FIG. 6–6. Typical installation at one of the Royal Canadian Air Force's Pine Tree radar warning line stations that uses a system containing an Orenda turbine to produce all electricity and heating requirements

Maintenance and Overhaul

In spite of the rapid growth of the gas turbine in a variety of applications, its characteristics and requirements are not broadly understood compared to the piston engine which is so thoroughly intermeshed in the daily life of everyone.

Factors Affecting Maintenance and Overhaul

The maintenance and overhaul requirements of the gas turbine engine, as for any type engine, are determined to a degree by the requirements of the individual installation. Likewise different makes and types of turbines will vary according to the design objectives.

The design goal for the compact or adapted aircraft type gas turbine engine necessitates compromises with respect to endurance life. Consequently, this engine generally requires more frequent and sophisticated inspection, maintenance, and overhaul. However, this disadvantage is, in part, offset by separable, easily handled subassemblies. These features permit the changing of engine components or even a complete engine replacement in a few hours. The larger industrial engines are generally serviced and overhauled at the facility where they are located. This overhaul usually requires shutdown of operations for a short period of time.

The primary factors directly related to engine maintenance and overhaul are duty cycle, quality of fuel, and environment and are described in the material which follows.

Duty Cycle

Hot section parts of the gas turbine engine are designed to operate over a wide temperature range. Inspection and maintenance requirements are, however, increased as thermal shock resulting from extreme load fluctuations is experienced.

Frequency of Start-Up. The number of starts may be considered a significant factor in the overall maintenance requirements. The more often a gas turbine engine starts and stops the more often the engine components are subjected to thermal cycles. Sometimes an engine start-up may produce temperatures higher than the normal operating temperatures. This so called "hot start" produces abnormal thermal stresses in the engine components.

Turbine Inlet Temperature. Generally, gas turbine engines are designed to operate at high temperature levels to gain maximum efficiency. The development and use of high-temperature alloys in recent years has greatly increased the life expectancy and performance of hot-section components. Hot section components include such items as the combustion chambers, transition liners, turbine nozzles, and blades. Overtemperature peaks and extended operation above the maximum recommended temperatures increase the requirements for inspection and repair for these components.

Overtemperature Recording. Thermal shock occurs to a degree during every engine start and every power (load) change. Therefore, it cannot be eliminated but it can be controlled by strict attention to the reduction of peak starting temperature. High thermal shocks are the responsibility of the operator, or the automatic control equipment. Recording of excessively hot gas stream temperatures, if they frequently occur, is very important with respect to proper inspection and maintenance. Prompt inspection following such malfunctions may prevent costly repairs.

Quality of Fuel

Natural or manufactured gases provide excellent fuels for gas turbine engines. Distillate or liquid fuels are also used and are readily available. In general, however, units burning gas or other clean gases will require less maintenance than the engines which utilize distillate type fuels.

It is important to note that liquid fuels and some gases contain corrosive and erosive contaminants which adversely affect engine life and performance. In an area where the constituents of the gas supply are unknown, the gas should be analyzed to determine the quantity and quality of contaminants which may harm engine components. Any fuel of questionable nature should be studied upon advice from the manufacturer of the particular engine.

Environment

The general environment of a gas turbine engine installation is not a critical factor if one assumes that proper maintenance procedures will be followed. The quality of the engine inlet air, however, is important. Airflow through the engine serves three major functions. Air is necessary for combustion, internal cooling, and mass flow through the turbine for the development of power. Contaminants in the engine air supply such as dust and smoke can be deposited in the engine and reduce engine efficiency. Abrasive particles which may pass through the engine tend to scar or erode rotor blades. Foreign chemicals in the air supply may be deposited on compressor components and they may cause corrosion or pitting of internal engine parts, especially the hot-section components.

Dirty compressor blading can cause loss of airflow and power as well as excessive starting temperature. The contamination that collects on compressor blades and vanes is usually the result of engine environment, but a malfunctioning component, such as a front oil seal, may also be the cause. Contamination normally builds up slowly. Therefore, the effect on engine performance is very gradual. However, the problem can be readily detected because of increasing peak starting temperatures and loss of output power.

Filters are usually placed in the compressor inlet air ducting to protect the engine from contaminants in the air. These commercial filters are readily available and will remove dust, smoke and other common contaminants as well as larger objects which may cause serious damage. Foreign deposits on components may be removed by injecting a cleaning agent such as commercially available ground walnut shells into the inlet air supply. Usually a dirty compressor cleaned with ground walnut shells will return the engine to normal operation if no other problems exist. In some cases, as much as 10% engine power loss can be regained by cleaning the compressor in this way without resorting to engine disassembly.

Turbine Operating Procedure

In the operation of a gas turbine the procedures may be described under the same classifications as for any prime mover, namely: Inspection, trouble shooting, repair, maintenance, overhaul, and factory unit-exchange and repair.

It is to be noted that each engine manufacturer has its own recommended practices, however, the general nature of the gas turbine operation is described under the appropriate headings in the material which follows.

Inspection

Routine inspections may include the usual examination of external lines, connections and engine mounts. Attention should be given to signs of engine vibration which may have caused visual damage. The gas turbine normally is not subject to the low frequency vibration expected in a reciprocating type engine; however, in case of foreign object damage to compressor or turbine blades, a very high frequency vibration may result. This type of vibration has a very small amplitude but can be very damaging due to the high frequency. It usually is prudent to maintain a continuous or frequent check for vibration with suitable engine instrumentation.

The first stage of compressor blading usually can be inspected for damage or dust accumulation rather easily. Certain industrial atmospheres may form an oily dust deposit which may cause a loss of power and an increase in fuel consumption. Blade erosion from sand particles may also be found.

The last stage of the turbine blading should be examined for possible damage and its condition may be indicative of the condition of other stages.

Combustion chambers, turbine inlet vanes, and fuel nozzles should be examined if the turbine temperatures are above normal. This may be caused by dirt in a fuel nozzle or turbine blading deterioration from overtemperature operation. It is important that a defective fuel nozzle be replaced promptly as serious damage can result from continuous overtemperature operation.

The engine may be rotated very slowly without fuel flow to examine for unnatural noises from the main bearings or excessive interference and rubbing of air seals.

Trouble Shooting

Some of the typical items of trouble shooting on gas turbines include the following:

Power Loss. Loss of power and high fuel consumption can be produced by dirt deposits on compressor blading from air-borne dust. This can be readily cleaned by introducing a cleaning material (usually ground walnut shells) into the compressor inlet while the engine is running. Damaged turbine blading can cause similar problems. Low turbine inlet temperature and low fuel flow may indicate a defective fuel control.

Vibration. High frequency vibration is checked with an instrument and is usually at the same frequency as engine rotation. Vibration may be caused by an excessive rubbing condition between a large diameter rotor and seal or between blade tips and a shroud. Vibration also results from out of balance conditions, which usually come from damaged blading in the turbine or compressor.

Turbine Inlet Temperature. Since the gas turbine is sensitive to excessive turbine inlet temperature it may be necessary on occasion to record the temperature during a starting cycle or to check the circumferential temperature distribution to determine if one nozzle or one combustion chamber is malfunctioning. The fuel control system may also require examination.

Failure to Start. A defective fuel control or lack of ignition are the usual reasons underlying failure to start. Most engines have two spark plugs for ignition even though there may be a greater number of combustion chambers. Only one spark plug is required to start the combustion and the flame then travels through cross-over tubes to all combustors.

Repair

Generally major components and accessories are readily accessible. Many designs are also adaptable to sectionalized repair techniques. Therefore, the repair can frequently be accomplished by replacing components or removing them to a repair or overhaul shop. On some engines it is possible to remove a portion of the casing and replace damaged blades at the installation site if only a limited number of blades are damaged. This is usually done by replacement of each blade with another blade having the same "moment-balance."

It is to be noted that all major assembly or component repair is a specialized operation and must be accomplished according to the engine manufacturer's specification.

Maintenance

A routine maintenance schedule is determined largely by experience and this experience factor is dependent largely on the duty cycle of the installation.

A general engine maintenance schedule is outlined as follows:

a. Clean air, oil and fuel filters.

b. Make electrical continuity check on magnetic oil drain plugs. This will determine if any foreign metallic material has been picked up from the oil.

c. Check turbine inlet temperature thermocouples for accuracy.

d. Electrical check of electronic control components.

e. Test igniter plugs.

f. Clean compressor blading with walnut shell treatment as determined by experience.

g. Check for engine vibration with appropriate instrumentation if preliminary examination shows any sign of excessive vibration.

h. Flow test fuel nozzles to assure proper flow rate and spray pattern.

Overhaul

The unique features in the overhaul of gas turbines include such operations as:

a. Precision balance of all high speed rotor assemblies.

b. Inspection for cracks in all highly stressed parts such as turbine and compressor blades and wheels, engine shafting, gears, welded joints, sheet metal assemblies, etc. Magnetic parts may be examined by magnetic particle inspection. Turbines have many non-magnetic stainless steel high temperature materials and they are examined by fluorescent penetrant inspection with ultra violet light.

c. Most turbines contain large diameter labyrinth seals which must be examined for excessive rubbing. These may require rework to remove burrs which have been raised from normal light rubbing.

d. A thorough check of electronic equipment usually used in fuel control systems is important to assure proper control of turbine inlet temperature.

Factory Unit-Exchange and Repair

Turbine engine production has reached a level where factory maintenance and overhaul services are common practice. These services provide the user with the technique approaching mass-production overhaul and an inventory of spare parts. Production type facilities enable the manufacturer to restore the engine to "new condition" in a minimum of time. Thorough inspection and production testing by experienced personnel provide prompt, reliable repair and overhaul, and relieve the user of the requirement for specialized equipment, a large inventory of spare parts, and highly skilled repair personnel.

CHAPTER 8

Estimating Gas Turbine Profitability

The major items to be considered in an economic analysis of a gas turbine installation are:

Cost of plant facilities
Amortization period
Interest on the investment
Salvage value of plant
Maintenance costs
Fuel costs
Operating labor costs
Taxes
Insurance
Miscellaneous supplies

When the owning and operating cost analysis of a gas turbine power plant has been completed, it then is necessary to compare this with the cost of purchased utilities for the various forms of energy produced by the plant. If this comparison indicates a favorable economic position for site-generated energy as compared to the purchase of plant energy requirements, then strong consideration should be given to the installation of the turbine power plant equipment.

Equipment Requirements

Generally, industrial and commercial buildings of the type where gas turbines are under consideration will have heavy requirements for electrical and heating energy in various forms. To produce the required forms of energy using a gas turbine system, it is necessary to provide electric generators and heat recovery equipment. In most of these plants, the electric generators will provide 60-cycle power; however, high frequency power (420 cps and higher) has distinct advantages in certain applications. These advantages are lower weight and less space for a given power output. As the use of high frequency power becomes more general, it is quite likely that on-site generation will provide the only economical means of producing this form of energy.

A survey of the plant electrical requirements should be made to determine the total connected electrical load, maximum anticipated electrical demand, daily, monthly, and annual consumption of electrical power and, most important for an accurate economic analysis, a load profile chart.

Quite often it is possible to eliminate one or two major electrical loads by substituting non-motor type prime movers. By the substitution of such equipment, it is possible to achieve improvement in the entire plant electrical load factors.

When due consideration has been given to the factors influencing power demand, thought then must be given to the total electrical plant requirements. Obviously, if site-generation is to be considered, the plant must have sufficient capacity to meet all demands placed upon it throughout its useful life. In practically all installations, this will require the purchase of equipment to meet the maximum plant demand with at least one additional generating unit for standby in case of unscheduled generator outage.

Heat Energy Requirements

The heat energy requirements of industrial plants and commercial buildings are a principal factor in the economics and vary considerably with the type of usage involved. For the turbine power plant to be economically feasible, the heating and cooling requirements of commercial buildings and light industrial plants must be sufficient to absorb a major portion of the available heat from the exhaust of the gas turbines which power electrical generators serving such buildings. The heat available, of course, will depend upon the turbine efficiency at the operating conditions. In what follows, it will be assumed that complete heating and comfort cooling will be provided for all buildings under consideration.

In some cases, however, heavy industrial plants require no cooling and only a minor amount of spot heating. In installations of this type, it often follows that the process heat requirements are considerably greater than the heat available from the exhaust gases of the gas turbine generating electrical power for the installation. If comfort heating and cooling constitute the major demand for heat energy, the heat from the turbine exhaust gas stream must be transferred to a more useful medium. Normally, this heat is transferred from the hot gas stream to water, thus producing steam in low pressure waste heat boilers. Although high pressure steam (above 15 psig) can be generated from the heat in the turbine exhaust stream at a high level of efficiency, the additional cost of utilization equipment for high pressure steam plus the higher labor cost of more capable operating personnel normally will make this type of equipment more expensive than that utilizing low pressure steam. In most cases studied to date, economic analyses have indicated that the lowest total owning and operating cost will be produced by use of low pressure steam-operated heating and absorption cooling equipment. In most communities, such equipment may be left unattended.

The maximum and average hourly heat energy requirements as well as peak day and annual heat energy requirements must be determined before an economic analysis can be completed. In the case of steam generation and other heat recovery equipment, the need for standby units is not so critical as it is in the case of electric generating equipment. Normally, the load factor of a commercial office building will be such that repairs to steam generating equipment can be accomplished during periods of low usage. In industrial installations, periods of slack usage or plant "turn around" normally will permit overhaul of steam generating equipment without loss of manufacturing capability.

Investment Costs and Charges

When comparing the relative merits of on-site generation of energy requirements versus the purchase of such energy from public utilities, it is necessary to determine the annual charges which accrue from the *net* additional investment required for on-site generation. In some cases, the cost of some items associated with the use of purchased energy may be deducted from the investment attributed to on-site generation. Some of these items are transformers, transformer vaults, underground power services, and electrical power hook-up charges.

The various components of the energy system must be amortized in accordance with accounting practices followed by the prospective purchaser, with particular attention being paid to practices permitted under Federal tax laws. As a rule, the cash flow generated by an energy system will be of considerable magnitude. In a situation of this type, it is desirable from the owner's standpoint to depreciate the plant equipment as rapidly as possible. Tables indicating the normal amortization period for various types of equipment which might be utilized in a gas turbine energy system are available.

During the amortization period of the equipment involved, the interest charged by lenders may vary considerably. The normal practice followed in determining interest rates to be charged on the capital investment is to assume that the then current rate of interest on available funds will be charged throughout the life of the plant.

As very few power plant components are operated to the end of their useful life, normal accounting procedures require the assignment of a salvage value to the various items of equipment at the end of the amortization period. This salvage value must be deducted from the total plant investment to determine the annual amount of depreciation charged off of the plant investment. It is difficult to assign a salvage value to the working components of any industrial plant, but an acceptable figure for tax purposes might range between 10% and 20%. The associated piping, wiring and other connective components generally are considered to have no more than junk value upon removal from the plant. In addition to the cost of plant machinery, additional charges for housing such machinery will be incurred. These must be included in the original plant investment. Taxes and insurance on the plant investment must be considered in the over-all cost of owning a plant.

Operation and Maintenance

Although the gas turbine has been in use for many years in aircraft and to a lesser degree in certain limited fields of stationary usage, there are no generally accepted rules which can be applied to all turbines for annual maintenance charges. To a large extent, these costs will be determined by the annual operating hours imposed upon the plant as well as by the degree of loading of the plant. For a specific installation, the manufacturers whose products are under consideration should be consulted for maintenance charges based on their current level of experience.

The cost of fuel will be one of the major charges incurred in any energy producing system. In what follows, it will be assumed that natural gas will provide a major portion of the total energy require- ments. It is important, however, to analyze the rate structures for all available sources of fuel to determine that combination of energy sources which produces the lowest annual fuel cost. Many gas util- ities have interruptible service rates which provide low cost off-peak gas rates, with the understanding that supplemental or standby fuel resources will be used by the customer during the utility's normal peak demand periods. If the interruptible type of rate provides sufficient discount from the firm rate, stand-by fuel supplies such as LPG or light fuel oil may be used instead of natural gas. Under such circum- stances, the user must purchase dual fuel firing equipment as well as fuel tanks and other items associated with the storage of the standby fuel.

System Analysis

An operating and economic analysis of a hypothetical office build- ing energy system follows. While the techniques employed here may be used in any analysis, *the data relating to hours of operation, fuel usage, fuel costs, labor costs and equipment costs must be obtained locally for use in analyzing a specific application.*

Energy System Example

The project is a 150,000 sq ft (floor area) office building in Austin, Texas. The load description is as follows:

Lighting and miscellaneous power load.

Weekdays	1200 kw, 6 am to 6 pm
Saturdays	600 kw, 6 am to 6 pm
Sundays	150 kw, 6 am to 6 pm
Night	150 kw, 6 pm to 6 am

Refrigeration load. Design temperature conditions 100 deg F dry bulb outside; 75 deg F dry bulb inside

Internal load (fixed), tons	360
Variable load (external plus outside air), tons	280
Total, tons	640

Table 8–1. Air Conditioning Power Requirements for Example Described in Text

Absorption System

	Per Cent of Full Load			
Item	100	75	50	25
	Kilowatts			
Chilled-hot water pump	32	32	32	32
Condenser water pump	49	49	49	49
Cooling tower fans	42	42	21	21
Chiller auxiliaries	12	10	10	10
Total	135	133	112	112

Electric Centrifugal System

	Kilowatts			
Chilled-hot water pump	32	32	32	32
Condenser water pump	38	38	38	38
Cooling tower fans	21	21	21	21
Chiller load	504	306	234	138
Total, KW	595	447	325	229

Absorption System

	Pounds per Hour			
Steam Requirements (Weekdays)	12,340	9,090	5,845	2,857

Gas Turbine System

	Kilowatts			
Power Produced	1,335	1,333	1,312	1,312
	Pounds per Hour			
Steam Produced	13,695	13,695	9,770	9,770
	Cubic Feet per Hour			
Gas Input	24,920	24,920	24,794	24,794

Heating load. Design temperature conditions 20 deg F dry bulb outside, 70 deg F dry bulb inside

Heating load at design conditions, Btu per hour   4,680,000
Heating load at 50 deg F, change-over point, Btu per hour
                                                          1,969,000

Water heating load. Approximately 58,500 gal per month, with an 80 deg F temperature rise. Approximately 50,000 cu ft per month gas consumption, with 80% combustion efficiency.

The air conditioning power requirements are shown in Table 8-1.

In addition to the data shown, the preparation of an operating analysis requires the development of local temperature information which normally is not available in a useful form. If heating and air conditioning utility usage is to be computed, it follows that the duration of temperatures affecting the load must be known. For illustrative purposes, the frequency of temperatures throughout the range encountered in Austin, Texas, is tabulated in Table 8-2.

By utilizing the load information described previously and the Energy System Analysis form which follows, the energy system loading

Table 8-2. Frequency of Occurrence of Various Temperatures in Austin, Texas (6 am to 6 pm)

Temperature, Deg F	Hours Per Year, Actual	Hours per Year		Refrigeration Load, Per-Cent
		Total	Weighted Basis*	
105	3 ⎫			
100	86 ⎬	411	294	100
95	322 ⎭			
90	373 ⎫			
85	398 ⎬	1,221	1,035	75
80	450 ⎭			
75	583 ⎫	1,035	994	50
70	452 ⎭			
65	420 ⎫			
60	350 ⎬	1,090	1,512	25
55	320 ⎭			
50	242	242	242	
45	207	207	207	
40	142	142	142	
35	80	80	80	
30	41	41	41	
25	8	8	8	
20	1	1	1	

* Weighted for loads under operation on weekday, Saturday and Sunday conditions, cooling only.

conditions at various temperatures can be determined for the typical use periods which are encountered in any commercial building. Since total load conditions for any given outside temperature will vary considerably among weekday, Saturday, Sunday, and nighttime operating conditions, it is desirable to establish weighted fuel consumption information for the various temperature conditions anticipated.

A similar procedure should be used for calculating the utility usage of the purchased power system.

How to Use the Energy System Analysis Form

Step 1. Fill in the basic data previously given under the heading "Building Data" in the upper portion of the form, shown in Fig. 8–1.

Step 2. Calculate the refrigeration load for the temperature conditions indicated in the bottom of the form, shown in Fig. 8–1. When the values for Normal Transmission, Solar, Outside Air and Internal Loads have been tabulated and totaled for the various conditions, it is possible to plot curves indicating the loads to be expected under these conditions. It has been assumed that an inside temperature of 75 deg will be satisfactory for most buildings, and this has been drawn as a horizontal line in the graph area on the left center portion of the form shown in Fig. 8–1. The inside design temperature may be altered at will. The use of 55 deg as a minimum temperature on the graph of operating conditions recognizes the fact that most air conditioning engineers prefer to use a ventilation cycle when the outside temperature falls below 55 deg in order to cut utility costs. These curves for the loading conditions provide a means of determining the refrigeration tonnage required at a given outside temperature for any of the typical operating conditions. For example, the curves plotted on the sample sheet indicate that temperatures falling between 90 and 100 deg correspond with refrigeration loads of:

Weekdays —87% to 100%
Saturdays —60% to 70%
Sundays   —30% to 40%

In a similar manner, the loading condition for other temperature ranges may be determined.

Step 3. From the curves and the data given in the statement of the operating conditions (Fig. 8–1), determine the power requirement of the system for each of the temperature ranges selected. In the sample problem, the 90 to 105 deg range was selected for the "100%"

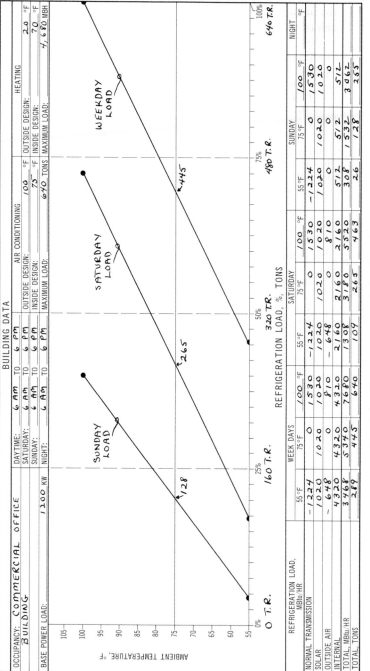

FIG. 8–1. Energy system analysis—Part 1

bracket. From the curves and the stated operating conditions, it is evident that the following loads will be imposed.

$$\text{Weekday} \quad —1,335 \text{ kw}$$
$$\text{Saturday} \quad — \ 733 \text{ kw}$$
$$\text{Sunday} \quad \ — \ 262 \text{ kw}$$

From the manufacturer's specification sheets, determine the fuel rate for each of these conditions and insert it in the appropriate space in the form shown in Fig. 8–2. As the load varies between weekdays, Saturdays and Sundays for any given temperature, a weighting factor must be applied to each of these unit fuel consumption figures to permit the development of a composite figure. Since "weekdays" constitute 5/7 of the total time, this fraction is used as a multiplier in arriving at the fuel usage increment charged to "weekday" operation. In like manner, Saturday and Sunday unit fuel consumptions are multiplied by 1/7 to determine the weighted input for these days. The total hourly fuel input is the sum of the inputs so developed. If the operating conditions of the project being analyzed do not follow the standard pattern used in this illustration, it is a simple matter to apply correct weighting factors to the unit fuel consumption figures.

Step 4. When the fuel consumption has been developed for all of the temperature ranges anticipated, these values should be inserted under "Fuel Usage, CF/HR" in Fig. 8–2 to the right opposite the appropriate temperature ranges as listed at the left of Fig. 8–2. For example, the composite fuel input for the 95 to 105 deg range is 21,115 cubic feet per hour. This was determined in Step 3. As illustrated on the sample form, a bracket has been drawn around these temperatures and 21,115 has been inserted opposite the bracket under the heading "Fuel Usage, CF/HR". In like manner, the values for fuel usage under other temperature range loadings may be inserted.

Step 5. The next step in the process is to determine the amount of exhaust heat available from the turbine exhaust at the selected loading conditions. This information may be obtained directly from the manufacturer's literature, or calculated if the exhaust gas temperature and mass flow are known. If it is determined that the turbine exhaust contains sufficient heat to meet the load requirements, there is no need for exhaust refiring calculations. However, if any of the stated load conditions do not provide sufficient exhaust heat to meet the load requirements, refiring will be necessary.

In the sample problem, the Saturday load for temperatures above 90 deg, the Sunday load for temperatures above 75 deg, and the Sunday heating load for temperatures below 45 deg indicate that the

POWER PLANT LOADING		POWER LOADING				EXHAUST HEAT AVAIL., MBtu/HR	HEAT REQUIRE-MENTS, MBtu/HR	EXHAUST REFIRING, MBtu/HR	TOTAL GAS INPUT, MBtu/HR	OPERATING TIME HR/MO/YR.	TOTAL GAS INPUT, MCF/MO/YR.
TEMP., °F / LOAD, %	BASE LOAD, KW	AIR COND., KW	AUX. LOAD, KW	TOTAL LOAD KW	FUEL INPUT, CF/KWH / FUEL USAGE, CF/HR						
110											
105											
100	1200	135	1	1335	21,115	12,700	11,900 (MAXIMUM)	453	21,568	411	8,864
95											
90	1200	133	1	1333	21,082	12,680		128	21,210	1221	27,382
85											
80											
75	1200	112	1	1312	20,941	12,650		NONE	20,941	1035	21,673
70											
65	1200	112	1	1312	20,941	12,650 (SUNDAY)		NONE (SUNDAY/7)	20,941	1090	22,846
60											
55											
50	1200	1	32	1232	18,875	2,780	1,969	25	18,875	247	4,567
45						18,875	2,780	2,460	95	18,900	207	3,907
40						18,875	2,780	2,954	165	18,970	142	2,683
35						18,875	2,780	3,442	165	19,040	80	1,517
30						18,875	2,780	3,930	187	19,062	41	780
25						18,875	2,780	4,192	270	19,145	8	152
20						18,875	2,780	4,680			1	19
15											
10											
5											
0											
−5											
NIGHT	150	1	32	182	4787				4787	4187	20,043
							TOTAL FUEL USAGE, MCF/YR.				114,433

*FUEL USAGE = (KW)(CF/KWH)(DAYS PER WEEK/7)

PERIOD (6 AM TO 6 PM)	TEMPERATURE RANGE: 105 °F TO 95 °F				TEMPERATURE RANGE: 90 °F TO 80 °F				TEMPERATURE RANGE: 75 °F TO 70 °F				TEMPERATURE RANGE: 65 °F TO 55 °F			
	LOAD, KW	FUEL RATE, CF/KWH	DAYS	FUEL* USAGE, CF/HR	LOAD, KW	FUEL RATE, CF/KWH	DAYS	FUEL* USAGE, CF/HR	LOAD, KW	FUEL RATE, CF/KWH	DAYS	FUEL* USAGE, CF/HR	LOAD, KW	FUEL RATE, CF/KWH	DAYS	FUEL* USAGE, CF/HR
WEEKDAYS	1335	18.66	5/7	17,795	1333	18.66	5/7	17,769	1312	18.8	5/7	17,699	1312	18.89	5/7	17,699
SATURDAY	735	23.65	1/7	2,484	233	23.65	1/7	2,477	712	23.65	1/7	2,406	712	23.65	1/7	2,406
SUNDAY	262	22.38	1/7	836	262	22.38	1/7	836	262	22.38	1/7	836	262	22.38	1/7	836
INPUT			CF/HR	21,115			CF/HR	21,082			CF/HR	20,941			CF/HR	20,941

FIG. 8-2. Energy system analysis—Part 2

steam produced will be insufficient to meet the load demands. Therefore, additional heat to be added by refiring must be calculated. It
should be noted that the high temperature of the exhaust gases permits refiring at combustion efficiencies up to 98%. Since these steam
deficiencies occur on Saturday and Sunday, the hourly deficiencies
should be divided by 7 to give the proper value for insertion in the
column labeled "Exhaust Refiring, MBtu/HR." After these values
have been inserted the next step can be considered.

Step 6. To obtain the "Total Gas Input, MBtu/HR," add the
values obtained for "Fuel Usage" and "Exhaust Refiring" for each
of the temperature ranges listed. From Table 8–2, obtain the monthly
or annual frequency of occurrence of each of the temperatures listed
and add them together to get the total number of hours in each range.
For purposes of simplicity, the sample problem has been solved on a
annual basis. It should be recognized that the complexities of utility
rate schedules usually require that fuel and power consumption be
listed on a monthly basis if accurate cost estimates are considered
desirable.

Step 7. To obtain "Total Gas Input" for the period under consideration, multiply the values of "Total Gas Input, MBtu/HR" by
"Operating Time, HRS/Month or Year" and divide the product by
1000. It is assumed in this case that each cubic foot of gas contains
1000 Btu, low heating value. Allowance should be made for any
substantial variation if it occurs. This can be done simply by multi-
plying with a factor found by dividing 1000 by the number of Btu's
actually contained in each cubic foot of gas.

Step 8. The total gas consumption for the period in question is
now obtained by adding the values obtained for each of the temperatures listed plus that obtained for night operation.

Cost of Operation of Purchased Power System

The development of power and gas consumption figures must be
completed before an objective analysis of the gas powered energy system is complete. For comparison purposes, the annual consumption
of electric power for Base Load Lights, Air Conditioning and Auxiliaries has been computed (See Table 8–1). In addition, the gas consumption for building heat and water heating was computed to permit
evaluation of the two systems on an equal basis. The electric load
when using purchased power can now be set up in the manner shown
in Table 8–3.

Table 8–3.   Electric Power Consumption, Purchased Power System

Temperature, Deg F.	Refrigeration Load, Per Cent	Refrigeration Load, kw	Hours Per Year, (Weighted)*	Power Usage, per Year
105 100 95	100	595	294	174,930
90 85 80	75	447	1,035	462,645
75 70	50	325	994	323,050
65 60 55	25	229	1,512	346,248
Hot Water Circulating Pump, 32 kw x 721 hours per year				23,072
Total Electric Load for Refrigeration				1,329,945

Base Load Power Consumption

Weekdays:	(1200 kw) (12 hr per day) (5) (52)	=	3,744,000
Saturdays:	(600 kw) (12 hr per day) (1) (52)	=	374,400
Sundays:	(150 kw) (12 hr per day) (1) (52)	=	93,600
Night:	(150 kw) (12 hr per day) (7) (52)	=	655,200

Base Load Total, kwh per year	4,867,200	4,867,200
Purchased Power Total Load, per year		6,197,145

* See Table 8–2

Table 8–4.   Cost of Equipment for Energy System and Purchased Power System

Quantity	Description	Purchased Power System, Dollars	Energy System, Dollars
5	500 hp 350 kw gas turbine generator units, $120 per kw	——	210,000
5	Exhaust heat boilers with boost burners, controls, at $10 per turbine horsepower	——	25,000
	Ducting and stacks	3,000	8,000
	Plant switchgear and panel, for generation only	——	30,000
2	Fuel gas compressor units, $5,000 each	——	10,000
1	Power transformer 1800 kw at $7 per kw	12,600	——
2	Boiler burner units at $8850 each	17,700	——
	Additional equipment space	——	5,000
	Total	$33,300	$288,000

Owning and Operating Cost

When the consumption of purchased utility services has been computed for both the energy system and the purchased power system, an estimate of first cost for the two systems can be worked up, as shown in Table 8–4. Following this, the important step of developing the comparison of annual cost, both owning and operating, can be calculated, as shown in Table 8–5. Cost data used for utility services, equipment, labor, and supplies vary from day to day so that the evaluation of a specific application must be based upon the use of current information. The data presented up to this point can now be sum-

Table 8–5. Annual Operating Expenses of the Two Systems

	Purchased Power System, Dollars	Energy System, Dollars
Taxes and Insurance, 2%	666	5,760
Maintenance		
Turbine-generator units 610 Kw-Yr continuous demand, at $4.80 per kw	——	2,934
Boilers Exhaust heat, 5 at $150 per yr	——	750
Gas fired, 2 at $200 per yr	400	——
Fuel gas compressor	——	500
Transformer	200	——
Fuel		
Power generation, heating and air conditioning, etc. 114,433 MCF per Yr at 25c per MCF	——	28,608
Building heat 8845 MCF 25 25c per MCF	2,211	——
Water heating 600 MCF at 25c per MCF	150	——
Purchased Power		
Base load: 4,867,200 kwh Heating and air conditioning: 1,329,945 kwh Total: 6,197,145 kwh at 1.75c per kwh	108,450	——
Water		
Electric refrigeration, 4300M-gallon at 30c per M gallons	1,290	——
Absorption refrigeration 8600 M-gallon at 30c per M gallons	——	2,580
Additional Labor		
2000 man-hours at $3.00 per man-hour	——	6,000
Total	$113,367	$47,132

marized as in Table 8–6, which contains all the information needed in the subsequent steps.

Table 8–6. Summary of Financial Data for the Two Systems

	Purchased Power System	Energy System
1. Initial investment in plant (Table 8–4)	$ 33,300	$288,000
2. Net plant investment for depreciation (initial investment less 10% salvage value)	29,970	259,200
3. Interest on initial investment (6%) (first year)	1,998	17,280
4. Annual operating cost (Table 8 –5)	113,367	47,132
5. Depreciation on net plant investment per year at 10% per year (line 2 x 10%)	2,997	25,920
6. Total annual owning and operating costs (first year) (lines 3, 4 and 5)	118,362	90,332
7. Net plant income from Energy System (See line 4: $113,365-$47,132)	——	66,235

The simplest method of calculating depreciation is on the straight line basis. This method is used in arriving at the year-by-year figures for the Energy System shown in Table 8–7.

Table 8–7. Profitability of Energy System as Indicated by Using Straight Line Depreciation

Year	Col. 1 Investment	Col. 2 Depreciation	Col. 3 Interest	Col. 4 Taxes, Ins., Maint., Labor, Fuel $	Col. 5 Annual Cost, Energy System $	Col. 6 Annual Cost for Purch. Power $	Col. 7 Annual Profit* $
1	$288,000	$ 25,920	$ 17,280	$ 47,132	$ 90,332	$113,367	$23,035
2	262,080	25,920	15,724	47,132	88,776	113,367	24,591
3	236,160	25,920	14,169	47,132	87,221	113,367	26,146
4	210,240	25,920	12,614	47,132	87,666	113,367	27,701
5	184,320	25,920	11,059	47,132	84,111	113,367	29,256
6	158,400	25,920	9,504	47,132	82,556	113,367	30,811
7	132,480	25,920	7,948	47,132	81,000	113,367	32,367
8	106,560	25,920	6,393	47,132	79,445	113,367	33,922
9	80,640	25,920	4,838	47,132	77,890	113,367	35,477
10	54,720	25,920	3,283	47,132	76,335	113,367	37,032
	$28,800†	$259,200	$102,812	$471,320	$833,332	$1,133,670	$300,338

† Salvage valve
* Before Federal Income Tax

It will be noticed that the data in Table 8–7 show a variable (increasing) profitability on a variable investment. In addition, the straight line method has the drawback of not taking into account the future value of the cash outlay required at the outset. The discounted Cash Flow method of analysis, which will be discussed later, overcomes this difficulty and provides a means of determining the profitability of a proposed project.

Determining the Cash Flow

Although a straight line depreciation schedule may be used in this type of analysis, the depreciation in Table 8–8, developed to show the Cash Flow, is based on a "sum-of-the-years digits" schedule. The sum-of-the-years digits method offers the advantage of quicker capital return plus increasing profits in the latter years when plant maintenance cost commences rising.

In the sum of the years digits method, a fraction is used in which the denominator d is $n/2$ $(n + 1)$ where n is the number of years over which the depreciation is taken. For example, if the depreciation period is 10 years, the denominator is $10/2$ $(10 + 1)$ = 55. During the first year the depreciation taken is n/d and each succeeding year the numerator is 1 less than that for the preceding year. In the 10 year example, the depreciation would be $10/55$ for the first year, $9/55$ the second, $8/55$ the third year and in 10 years these would total $55/55$.

In Table 8–8, Col. 2 is from Table 8–6, and Col. 4 is this figure multiplied by the years digits shown in Col. 3. Col. 5 shows the

Table 8–8. Cash Flow Statement, Using Sum-of-the-Years Digits Method of Calculating Depreciation

Col. 1	Col. 2	Col. 3		Col. 4	Col. 5	Col. 6	Col. 7	Col. 8
Year	Net Plant Income	Depreciation of Net Plant Investment of $259,200			Balance of Deprec. at End of Year	Federal Income Tax	Profit	Cash Flow
		Fraction	Dollars					
0	0	0		0	$259,200	0	0	—254,700
1	$66,235	10/55		$47,127	212,073	$ 9,936	$ 9,172	56,299
2	66,235	9/55		42,415	169,658	12,386	11,434	53,849
3	66,235	8/55		37,702	131,956	14,837	13,696	51,398
4	66,235	7/55		32,989	98,967	17,288	15,958	48,947
5	66,235	6/55		28,276	70,961	19,738	18,221	46,497
6	66,235	5/55		23,564	47,127	22,189	20,482	44,046
7	66,235	4/55		18,851	28,276	24,639	22,745	41,596
8	66,235	3/55		14,138	14,138	27,090	25,007	39,145
9	66,235	2/55		9,425	4,713	29,541	27,269	36,694
10	66,235	1/55		4,713	0	31,991	29,531	34,244
	$662,350	55/55		$259,200		$209,635	$193,515	$198,015

balance remaining to be depreciated at the end of the year after deducting the value in Col. 4. The difference between Col. 2 and Col. 4 is the profit before Federal taxes (not shown) and this figure, multiplied by .52 gives the Federal income tax (Col. 6), the remainder being profit (Col. 7). The Cash Flow (Col. 8) is then the income less the Federal tax (Col. 2 — Col. 6) or the sum of the depreciation and the profit (Col. 4 + Col. 7).

It should be noted in Table 8–8 that the initial cash flow (Col. 8) begins with $254,700 (not $259,200). The figure of $254,700 is the initial cash outflow for the Energy System ($288,000) less the initial cost of the Purchased Power System ($33,300).

The Discounted Cash Flow analysis may be used whether the proposed plant is to be built with borrowed funds, retained earnings, or capital obtained through the sale of debt or equity securities. Its primary purpose is to indicate the relative profitability of various projects in which a firm might invest available funds, and by applying "present value" discounts to the cash flow obtained from the operation of the project one may determine the rate of profit returned by the project.

When the cash flow statement has been prepared, then the profitability of the project may be determined on a trial and error basis. The profitability may be defined as the project's effective annual earnings, expressed as a percent of the outstanding capital invested. The profitability rate is the discount rate which will cause the cash flow to diminish to a zero present value. A table of discount factors which gives the present value of an amount equal to $1 considered some period hence at various rates of annually compounded interest is included as Table 8–9.

Table 8–9. Discount Factors for Use in Calculating Discounted Cash Flow†

Period	8%	10%	12%	14%	16%	18%	20%	22%	24%
	Income Received at an Instant of Time								
0	1.0000	1.0000	1.0000	1.0000	1.0000	1.0000	1.0000	1.0000	1.0000
1	0.9259	0.9091	0.8928	0.8772	0.8621	0.8475	0.8333	0.8197	0.8065
2	0.8573	0.8264	0.7972	0.7695	0.7431	0.7182	0.6944	0.6719	0.6504
3	0.7938	0.7513	0.7118	0.6750	0.6407	0.6086	0.5787	0.5507	0.5245
4	0.7350	0.6830	0.6355	0.5921	0.5523	0.5158	0.4823	0.4514	0.4230
5	0.6806	0.6209	0.5674	0.5194	0.4761	0.4371	0.4019	0.3700	0.3411
6	0.6302	0.5645	0.5066	0.4556	0.4104	0.3704	0.3349	0.3033	0.2751
7	0.5835	0.5132	0.4523	0.3996	0.3538	0.3139	0.2791	0.2486	0.2218
8	0.5403	0.4665	0.4039	0.3506	0.3050	0.2660	0.2326	0.2038	0.1789
9	0.5002	0.4241	0.3606	0.3075	0.2630	0.2255	0.1938	0.1670	0.1443
10	0.4632	0.3855	0.3220	0.2697	0.2267	0.1911	0.1615	0.1369	0.1164
11	0.4289	0.3505	0.2875	0.2366	0.1954	0.1619	0.1346	0.1122	0.0938
12	0.3971	0.3186	0.2567	0.2076	0.1685	0.1372	0.1122	0.0920	0.0757
13	0.3677	0.2897	0.2292	0.1821	0.1452	0.1163	0.0935	0.0754	0.0610
14	0.3405	0.2633	0.2046	0.1597	0.1252	0.0985	0.0779	0.0618	0.0492
15	0.3152	0.2394	0.1827	0.1401	0.1079	0.0835	0.0649	0.0507	0.0397
16	0.2919	0.2176	0.1631	0.1229	0.0930	0.0708	0.0541	0.0415	0.0320
17	0.2703	0.1978	0.1456	0.1078	0.0802	0.0600	0.0451	0.0340	0.0258
18	0.2502	0.1799	0.1300	0.0946	0.0691	0.0508	0.0376	0.0279	0.0208
19	0.2317	0.1635	0.1161	0.0829	0.0596	0.0431	0.0313	0.0229	0.0168
20	0.2145	0.1486	0.1037	0.0728	0.0514	0.0365	0.0261	0.0187	0.0135
21	0.1987	0.1351	0.0926	0.0638	0.0443	0.0309	0.0217	0.0154	0.0109
22	0.1839	0.1228	0.0826	0.0560	0.0382	0.0262	0.0181	0.0126	0.0088
23	0.1703	0.1117	0.0738	0.0491	0.0329	0.0222	0.0151	0.0103	0.0071
24	0.1577	0.1015	0.0659	0.0431	0.0284	0.0188	0.0126	0.0085	0.0057
25	0.1460	0.0923	0.0588	0.0378	0.0245	0.0160	0.0105	0.0069	0.0046

† Reproduced by permission of Financial Publishing Co., 82 Brookline Ave., Boston, Mass.

Values for this table are computed from the following compound interest formula:

$$V = \frac{P}{(1 + r)^n}$$

where V is the present value of an amount P due or considered in n number of years at an interest rate of r. For the purposes of this table P is taken equal to $1 and considering the formula in the form $V = P\left[\dfrac{1}{(1 + r)^n}\right]$, any factor in the table is the numerical value of the expression contained within the brackets corresponding to an interest rate r and n number of years. For example, if the interest rate is 10% and n, the number of years, is 15, then $\left[\dfrac{1}{(1 + r)^n}\right] = .2394$. With P always being equal to $1, then $V = \$1\,[.2394] = \$.2394$ or $\$.2394$ is the present value of $1 considered 15 years from now at an interest rate of 10%.

In summarizing then, for the purposes of this discussion, the factors in Table 8–9 are the present value of what will be 1, n years from now at a certain rate of interest.

Table 8–10 is a Discounted Cash Flow Statement. In this table, Col. 2 is the Cash Flow previously determined and shown in Col. 8

Table 8-10.   Discounted Cash Flow Statement

Year	Cash Flow	Discount Factor, 12%	Discounted Cash Flow, 12%	Discount Factor, 14%	Discounted Cash Flow, 14%
0	—$254,700	1.0000	—$254,700	1.0000	—$254,700
1	56,299	.8928	50,263	.8772	49,385
2	53,849	.7972	42,928	.7695	41,437
3	51,398	.7118	36,585	.6750	34,694
4	48,497	.6355	31,106	.5921	28,982
5	46,497	.5674	26,382	.5194	24,151
6	44,046	.5066	22,314	.4556	20,067
7	41,596	.4523	18,814	.3996	16,622
8	39,145	.4039	15,810	.3506	13,724
9	36,694	.3606	13,232	.3075	11,283
10	34,244	.3220	11,027	.2697	9,236
	$198,015		$13,761		—$5,119

Interpolation:

$$\text{Profitability Rate} = \left(\frac{13761}{13761 + 5119}\right)(14 - 12) + 12$$

$$= 1.458 + 12$$

$$\text{Profitability} = 13.46\%$$

of Table 8–8. By trial and error, it is found that the end of the 10 year period a positive remainder is found for the 12% rate, using Table 8–9 and a negative remainder when using 14%. Thus the two remainders "straddle" the actual interest rate, or profitability.

In Table 8–10, Col. 3 is the factor for the year shown in Col. 1 under 12% in Table 8–9. For example, in Table 8–9, for 12% and 7 years, the factor is 0.4523. This appears, then, in Table 8–10 opposite 7 years, and these factors are multiplied by the cash flow in Col. 2, arriving at the discounted cash flow.

Since the remainder in Table 8–10 is positive in one case, negative in another, interpolation is made to determine exactly where between 12% and 14% the profitability lies. The computation of this rate is shown at the bottom of Table 8–10 to be 13.46%.

In this case, the sole purpose of using the Discounted Cash Flow Method and Table 8–10 was to determine profitability. The actual accounting later employed would probably be somewhat as indicated in Table 8–8.

Additional income from tenant purchases of power, heating and air conditioning energy would have increased the annual income of this project, thus increasing its profitability rate. Had the same system been analyzed for a more favorable location requiring greater volumes of steam, maximum exhaust heat utilization and subsequent refiring would have produced a higher profitability rate. The low load factor and slightly unbalanced load conditions of the sample problem reduced profits, but the results still indicate a most attractive return on the investor's dollar.

Summary

From this analysis it should be evident that the gas turbine energy system is capable of producing respectable profits for the investor even under adverse circumstances. In those cases where operating conditions combine favorably, its shaft-heat energy capabilities provide exceedingly good profit potential.

Appendix

Formula for Determining Correction Factor for Gas Volume when Gas Temperature is other than 60 deg F and Total Gas Pressure is other than 30.0 in. Hg

$$\text{Correction factor, F} = \frac{519.7}{459.7 + t} \times \frac{P - w_t}{29.4782}$$

where:
    P = total gas pressure in inches of mercury,
    w_t = saturated vapor pressure of water, at temperature t, in inches of mercury, and
    t = gas temperature in degrees Fahrenheit

Temperature Conversion Formulas

Conversion of deg F to deg C or deg C to deg F requires the following sequence of three steps:

1. Add 40 deg to the value.
2. Multiply result by either 9/5 to convert to deg F or 5/9 to convert to deg C.
3. Subtract 40 from this result.

$$°R = °F \text{ abs} = \text{deg Rankine} = °F + 460°$$
$$°K = °C \text{ abs} = \text{deg Kelvin} = °C + 273°$$
$$°\text{Celsius*} = 0.01 \text{ deg} + (.9999 \times \text{deg C})$$
$$°\text{Reaumur} = 0.8° \text{ Centigrade}$$

* The base of the Celsius scale is the triple point (solid, liquid, and gas in equilibrium) of water which is at 0.01 Centigrade.

Combustion Characteristics of Chemical Compounds

Fuel	Specific volume cu ft/lb	Theoretical air required cu ft/cu ft	Theoretical air required cu ft/lb	Gross Btu per cu ft std air	Ultimate percent CO_2	Products of perfect combustion* CO_2	H_2O	N_2	SO_2	Total
Carbon (C)	...	...	151.3	93.0	20.9	3.67	0	8.85	0	12.52
Hydrogen (H_2)	187.7	2.39	453	135.0	...	**0**	**1.00**	**1.89**	**0**	**2.89**
						0	9.00	26.60	0	35.60
Sulfur (S)	...	...	56.7	70.3	...	0	0	3.32	2.00	5.32
Carbon monoxide (CO)	13.51	2.39	32.5	133.7	34.6	**1.00**	**0**	**1.89**	**0**	**2.89**
						1.57	0	1.90	0	3.47
Hydrogen sulfide (H_2S)	10.98	7.17	78.5	95.3	...	**0**	**1.00**	**5.67**	**1.00**	**7.67**
						0	0.53	4.68	1.88	7.09
Methane (CH_4)	23.61	9.56	226.5	105.4	11.68	**1.00**	**2.00**	**7.56**	**0**	**10.56**
						2.75	2.25	13.28	0	18.28
Ethane (C_2H_6)	12.50	16.72	212.0	105.2	13.15	**2.00**	**3.00**	**13.22**	**0**	**18.22**
						2.96	1.80	12.40	0	17.16
Propane (C_3H_8)	8.45	23.9	206.5	104.9	13.70	**3.00**	**4.00**	**18.90**	**0**	**25.90**
						3.00	1.64	12.07	0	16.71
Butane (C_4H_{10})	6.29	31.1	203.5	104.7	14.00	**4.00**	**5.00**	**24.60**	**0**	**33.60**
						3.04	1.55	11.90	0	16.49
Octane (C_8H_{18})	...	...	199.0	103.5	14.42	3.09	1.42	11.67	0	16.18
Acetylene (C_2H_2)	14.54	11.95	176.7	122.1	17.46	**2.00**	**1.00**	**9.45**	**0**	**12.45**
						3.38	0.69	10.22	0	14.29

* Boldface figures are in cu ft/cu ft of fuel; lightface figures are in lb/lb of fuel.

From The North American Mfg. Co.'s Combustion Handbook

Equations for Determining Products of Combustion of Gaseous Fuels (all percentages are percents by volume)

$$\frac{\text{lb comb prod}}{\text{cu ft fuel}} = \%CO \times 0.00256 + \%H_2 \times 0.001873 + \%CH_4 \times 0.00772 + \%C_2H_6 \times 0.01356 + \%C_3H_8 \times 0.0194 + \%C_4H_{10} \times 0.0261 + \%CO_2 \times 0.001164 + \%N_2 \times 0.00074 + \%H_2O \times 0.000476 - \%O_2 \times 0.0028$$

$$\frac{\text{lb } CO_2}{\text{cu ft fuel}} = \%CO \times 0.001165 + \%CH_4 \times 0.001165 + \%C_2H_6 \times 0.00230 + \%C_3H_8 \times 0.00349 + \%C_4H_{10} \times 0.00465 + \%CO_2 \times .001164$$

$$\frac{\text{lb } H_2O}{\text{cu ft fuel}} = \%H_2 \times 0.000476 + \%CH_4 \times 0.000951 + \%C_2H_6 \times 0.00143 + \%C_3H_8 \times 0.001905 + \%C_4H_{10} \times 0.00238 + \%H_2O \times 0.000476$$

$$\frac{\text{lb } N_2}{\text{cu ft fuel}} = \%CO \times 0.001398 + \%H_2 \times 0.001398 + \%CH_4 \times 0.00561 + \%C_2H_6 \times 0.00980 + \%C_3H_8 \times 0.01398 + \%C_4H_{10} \times 0.01821 + \%N_2 \times 0.00074 - \%O_2 \times 0.0028$$

$$\frac{\text{cu ft comb prod}}{\text{cu ft fuel}} = \%CO \times 0.0289 + \%H_2 \times 0.0289 + \%CH_4 \times 0.1056 + \%C_2H_6 \times 0.1824 + \%C_3H_8 \times 0.2590 + \%C_4H_{10} \times 0.3360 + \% \text{ inerts} \times 0.01 - \%O_2 \times 0.0378$$

$$\frac{\text{cu ft dry comb prod}}{\text{cu ft fuel}} = \%CO \times 0.0289 + \%H_2 \times 0.0189 + \%CH_4 \times 0.0856 + \%C_2H_6 \times 0.1524 + \%C_3H_8 \times 0.2190 + \%C_4H_{10} \times 0.2860 + \% \text{ inerts} \times 0.01 - \%O_2 \times 0.0378$$

$$\frac{\text{cu ft } CO_2}{\text{cu ft fuel}} = \%CO \times 0.01 + \%CH_4 \times 0.01 + \%C_2H_6 \times 0.02 + \%C_3H_8 \times 0.03 + \%C_4H_{10} \times 0.04 + \%CO_2 \times 0.01$$

$$\%CO_2 \text{ in dry flue gases} = 100 \times \frac{\text{cu ft } CO_2}{\text{cu ft fuel}} \div \frac{\text{cu ft dry comb prod}}{\text{cu ft fuel}}$$

$$\frac{\text{cut ft } H_2O}{\text{cu ft fuel}} = \%H_2 \times 0.01 + \%CH_4 \times 0.02 + \%C_2H_6 \times 0.03 + \%C_3H_8 \times 0.04 + \%C_4H_{10} \times 0.05 + \%H_2O \times 0.01$$

$$\frac{\text{cu ft } N_2}{\text{cu ft fuel}} = \%CO \times 0.0189 + \%H_2 \times 0.0189 + \%CH_4 \times 0.0756 + \%C_2H_6 \times 0.1324 + \%C_3H_8 \times 0.1890 + \%C_4H_{10} \times 0.2460 + \%N_2 \times 0.01 - \%O_2 \times 0.0378$$

From The North American Mfg. Co.'s Combustion Handbook

Equations for Determining Products of Combustion of Liquid and Solid Fuels (all percentages are percents by weight)

$$\frac{\text{lb comb prod}}{\text{lb fuel}} = \%C \times 0.1253 + \%H \times 0.356 + \%S \times 0.053 + \%\text{ inerts} + 0.01 - \%O \times 0.0332$$

$$\frac{\text{lb } CO_2}{\text{lb fuel}} = \%C \times 0.0367 + \%CO_2{}^* \times 0.01$$

$$\frac{\text{lb } H_2O}{\text{lb fuel}} = \%H \times 0.09 + \%H_2O\dagger \times 0.01$$

$$\frac{\text{lb } N_2}{\text{lb fuel}} = \%C \times 0.0886 + \%H \times 0.2658 + \%S \times 0.033 + \%N \times 0.01 - \%O \times 0.0332$$

$$\frac{\text{cu ft comb prod}}{\text{lb fuel}} = \%C \times 1.505 + \%H \times 5.46 + \%S \times 0.557 + \%CO_2{}^* \times 0.0859 + \%H_2O\dagger \times 0.21 + \%N \times 0.135 - \%O \times 0.448$$

$$\frac{\text{cu ft dry prod}}{\text{lb fuel}} = \%C \times 1.505 + \%H \times 3.57 + \%S \times 0.557 + \%CO_2{}^* \times 0.0859 + \%N \times 0.135 - \%O \times 0.448$$

$$\frac{\text{cu ft } CO_2}{\text{lb fuel}} = \%C \times 0.315 + \%CO_2{}^* \times 0.0859$$

$$\%CO_2 \text{ in dry flue gases} = 100 \times \frac{\text{cu ft } CO_2}{\text{lb fuel}} \div \frac{\text{cu ft dry comb prod}}{\text{lb fuel}}$$

$$\frac{\text{cu ft } H_2O}{\text{lb fuel}} = \%H \times 1.89 + \%H_2O\dagger \times 0.21$$

$$\frac{\text{cu ft } N_2}{\text{lb fuel}} = \%C \times 1.046 + \%H \times 3.14 + \%S \times 0.392 + \%N \times 0.135 - \%O \times 0.448$$

NOTES: *a.* These equations may be used for gaseous fuels which contain no CO.

b. If the values substituted in the above equations for %C and %H are the percentages of total carbon and hydrogen (available plus unavailable), then the %O should be the total (free and combined) oxygen.

c. If the values substituted in the above equations for %C and %H are the percentages of available carbon and hydrogen respectively, then the %O should be the free oxygen only.

* If %C includes the unavailable carbon already in the form of CO_2, this CO_2 term may be omitted.

† If %H includes the unavailable hydrogen already in the form of H_2O, this H_2O term may be omitted.

From The North American Mfg. Co.'s Combustion Handbook

Conversions for Standard Gas Conditions

To convert from	To	Multiply by
Btu per cubic foot 60°F and 30 in. Hg dry	Calories per cubic meter 0°C and 760 mm Hg dry	9.377
Btu per cubic foot 60°F and 30 in. Hg saturated	Calories per cubic meter 0°C and 760 mm Hg dry	9.549
Btu per cubic foot 60°F and 30 in. Hg saturated	Calories per cubic meter 0°C and 760 mm Hg saturated	9.490
Calories per cubic meter 0°C and 760 mm Hg saturated	Btu per cubic foot 60°F and 30 in. Hg saturated	0.1054
Calories per cubic meter 0°C and 760 mm Hg dry	Btu per cubic foot 60°F and 30 in. Hg saturated	0.1047
Cubic feet 60°F and 30 in. Hg saturated	Cubic meters 0°C and 760 mm Hg dry	0.0264
Cubic feet 60°F and 30 in. Hg saturated	Cubic meters 0°C and 760 mm Hg saturated	0.0266
Cubic meters 0°C and 760 mm Hg dry	Cubic feet 60°F and 30 in. Hg saturated	37.887
Cubic meters 0°C and 760 mm Hg saturated	Cubic feet 60°F and 30 in. Hg saturated	37.656
Btu per pound	Calories per kilogram	0.5556
Calories per kilogram	Btu per pound	1.8000

Industrial-Commercial Gas Pipe Sizes, Various Pressures

Industrial-Commercial Gas Pipe Sizes, Pressures Under 1 Lb.

(Pressure drop, 0.5 in. of water, specific gravity of gas, 0.60)

Diameter of Pipe, Inches (IPS)	Total Equivalent Length of Pipe, Feet									
	50	100	150	200	250	300	400	500	1000	1500
	Capacity in Cubic Feet per Hour									
1	244	173	141	122	109	99	86	77	54	44
1¼	537	380	310	268	240	219	189	169	119	97
1½	832	588	480	416	372	339	294	263	185	151
2	1,680	1,188	970	840	751	685	594	531	375	306
2½	2,754	1,952	1,591	1,379	1,232	1,123	974	869	617	504
3	5,018	3,549	2,896	2,509	2,244	2,047	1,774	1,587	1,121	915
4	8,464	5,986	4,885	4,232	3,785	3,454	2,992	2,677	1,891	1,544
5	14,595	10,323	8,425	7,298	6,527	5,956	5,160	4,616	3,262	2,663
6	22,472	15,894	12,972	11,238	10,050	9,170	7,945	7,108	5,022	4,101
8	41,516	29,364	23,965	20,760	18,567	16,943	14,679	13,132	9,279	7,577

Industrial-Commercial Gas Pipe Sizes, 1 Lb. Pressure

(For an initial pressure of 1 psig, a pressure drop of 0.1 psi and gas of 0.60 specific gravity)

Diameter of Pipe, Inches (IPS)	Total Equivalent Length of Pipe, Feet									
	50	100	150	200	300	400	500	1000	1500	2000
	Capacity in Cubic Feet per Hour									
1	740	520	430	370	300	260	230	170	130	120
1¼	1,540	1,090	890	760	630	540	490	350	280	250
1½	2,330	1,650	1,350	1,160	960	830	740	530	420	380
2	4,550	3,210	2,640	2,260	1,870	1,610	1,440	1,040	830	750
2½	7,330	5,180	4,250	3,650	3,020	2,600	2,320	1,690	1,340	1,200
3	13,100	9,260	7,600	6,520	5,400	4,660	4,160	3,020	2,400	2,160
3½	19,320	13,650	11,210	9,610	7,960	6,870	6,130	4,430	3,540	3,180
4	26,980	19,070	15,650	13,430	11,120	9,590	8,560	6,220	4,940	4,440
5	49,340	34,870	28,620	24,550	20,330	17,550	15,660	11,370	9,030	8,130
6	80,560	56,940	46,740	40,090	33,210	28,650	25,580	18,570	14,760	13,280

Industrial-Commercial Gas Pipe Sizes, 2 Lb. Pressure

(For an initial pressure of 2 psig, a pressure drop of 0.2 psi and gas of 0.60 specific gravity)

Diameter of Pipe, Inches (IPS)	Total Equivalent Length of Pipe, Feet									
	50	100	150	200	300	400	500	1000	1500	2000
	Capacity in Cubic Feet per Hour									
1	1,080	760	620	540	440	380	340	240	190	170
1¼	2,250	1,590	1,300	1,120	910	790	710	500	410	350
1½	3,410	2,410	1,970	1,700	1,390	1,200	1,070	760	620	530
2	6,640	4,700	3,840	3,310	2,700	2,350	2,090	1,480	1,210	1,040
2½	10,700	7,580	6,190	5,340	4,360	3,790	3,380	2,390	1,960	1,690
3	19,120	13,540	11,060	9,610	7,790	6,770	6,040	4,280	3,500	3,020
3½	28,200	19,970	16,310	14,070	11,490	9,980	8,900	6,310	5,160	4,450
4	39,380	27,890	22,780	19,650	16,040	13,940	12,440	8,810	7,210	6,220
5	72,010	50,990	41,650	35,930	29,300	25,490	22,740	16,120	13,180	11,370
6	117,580	83,270	68,010	58,670	47,900	41,630	37,140	26,320	21,520	18,570

Industrial-Commercial Gas Pipe Sizes, Various Pressures (*Continued*)

Industrial-Commercial Gas Pipe Sizes, 5 Lb. Pressure

(For an initial pressure of 5 psig, a pressure drop of 0.5 psi and gas of 0.60 specific gravity)

Diameter of Pipe, Inches (IPS)	Total Equivalent Length of Pipe, Feet									
	50	100	150	200	300	400	500	1000	1500	2000
	Capacity in Cubic Feet per Hour									
1	1,860	1,320	1,070	930	760	660	590	410	340	290
1¼	3,870	2,740	2,240	1,930	1,580	1,370	1,220	860	700	610
1½	5,860	4,140	3,390	2,930	2,390	2,080	1,850	1,310	1,060	930
2	11,420	8,070	6,600	5,710	4,660	4,050	3,610	2,550	2,080	1,810
2½	18,400	13,010	10,640	9,200	7,510	6,530	5,820	4,110	3,350	2,920
3	32,860	23,240	19,000	16,430	13,410	11,660	10,390	7,340	5,990	5,220
3½	48,480	34,280	28,030	24,240	19,780	17,200	15,330	10,820	8,840	7,690
4	67,700	47,880	39,140	33,850	27,630	24,020	21,410	15,120	12,340	10,750
5	123,790	87,540	71,570	61,890	50,530	43,920	39,160	27,640	22,570	19,660
6	202,138	142,950	116,870	101,060	82,500	71,720	63,940	45,140	36,860	32,100

Industrial-Commercial Gas Pipe Sizes, 10 Lb. Pressure

(For an initial pressure of 10 psig, a pressure drop of 1 psi and gas of 0.60 specific gravity)

Diameter of Pipe, Inches (IPS)	Total Equivalent Length of Pipe, Feet									
	50	100	150	200	300	400	500	1000	1500	2000
	Capacity in Cubic Feet per Hour									
1	2,930	2,070	1,690	1,470	1,190	1,030	920	650	530	460
1¼	6,090	4,330	3,520	3,050	2,490	2,150	1,920	1,360	1,110	960
1½	9,210	6,530	5,330	4,620	3,760	3,260	2,910	2,060	1,680	1,460
2	17,940	12,720	10,380	9,000	7,330	6,360	5,680	4,020	3,280	2,840
2½	28,920	20,500	16,730	14,510	11,820	10,250	9,150	6,480	5,290	4,580
3	51,650	36,610	29,880	25,920	21,110	18,300	16,340	11,570	9,450	8,190
3½	76,180	53,990	44,070	38,240	31,140	26,990	24,110	17,070	13,950	12,080
4	106,400	75,410	61,550	53,410	43,500	37,700	33,670	23,850	19,480	16,870
5	194,540	137,890	112,550	97,650	79,540	68,940	61,570	43,600	35,620	30,860
6	317,650	225,150	183,770	159,450	129,870	112,560	100,540	71,200	58,160	50,390

Industrial-Commercial Gas Pipe Sizes 20 Lb. Pressure

(For an initial pressure of 20 psig, a pressure drop of 2 psi and gas of 0.60 specific gravity)

Diameter of Pipe, Inches (IPS)	Total Equivalent Length of Pipe, Feet									
	50	100	150	200	300	400	500	1000	1500	2000
	Capacity in Cubic Feet per Hour									
1	4,900	3,470	2,810	2,450	2,000	1,730	1,550	1,070	890	770
1¼	10,190	7,210	5,840	5,090	4,160	3,600	3,220	2,230	1,860	1,610
1½	15,420	10,900	8,830	7,710	6,290	5,450	4,870	3,370	2,810	2,440
2	30,030	21,230	17,190	15,010	12,260	10,610	9,490	6,570	5,480	4,760
2½	48,390	34,220	27,710	24,190	19,750	17,110	15,290	10,590	8,830	7,670
3	86,420	61,110	49,490	43,190	35,280	30,550	27,310	18,910	15,770	13,690
3½	127,480	90,130	73,000	63,710	52,040	45,070	40,280	27,900	23,270	20,200
4	178,040	125,880	101,950	88,980	72,680	62,940	56,260	38,960	32,500	28,210
5	325,530	230,170	186,410	162,700	132,890	115,080	102,870	71,240	59,420	51,590
6	531,530	375,820	304,370	265,660	216,990	187,910	167,980	116,330	97,030	84,240

Industrial-Commercial Gas Pipe Sizes, Various Pressures (*Continued*)

Industrial-Commercial Gas Pipe Sizes, 50 Lb. Pressure

(For an initial pressure of 50 psig, a pressure drop of 5 psi and gas of 0.60 specific gravity)

Diameter of Pipe, Inches (IPS)	Total Equivalent Length of Pipe, Feet									
	50	100	150	200	300	400	500	1000	1500	2000
	Capacity in Cubic Feet per Hour									
1	10,530	7,450	6,090	5,150	4,350	3,790	3,330	2,350	1,920	1,650
1¼	21,880	15,490	12,650	10,700	9,050	7,870	6,920	4,890	3,990	3,430
1½	33,110	23,430	19,130	16,190	13,690	11,910	10,470	7,410	6,040	5,190
2	64,450	45,610	37,250	31,530	26,660	23,190	20,400	14,420	11,770	10,110
2½	103,870	73,510	60,040	50,820	42,960	37,370	32,870	23,240	18,970	16,300
3	185,490	131,270	107,220	90,750	76,720	66,730	58,700	41,510	33,870	29,100
3½	273,600	193,620	158,140	133,850	113,170	98,430	86,590	61,230	49,970	42,930
4	382,110	270,420	220,870	186,940	158,050	137,480	120,930	85,510	69,780	59,960
5	698,660	494,430	403,840	341,800	288,980	251,360	221,110	156,360	127,600	109,630
6	1,140,780	807,320	659,400	558,110	471,860	410,430	361,040	255,310	208,340	179,010

Multipliers to be Used with Preceding Table when the Specific Gravity of the Gas is other than 0.60

Specific Gravity	Multiplier	Specific Gravity	Multiplier
.35	1.31	1.00	.775
.40	1.23	1.10	.740
.45	1.16	1.20	.707
.50	1.10	1.30	.680
.55	1.04	1.40	.655
.60	1.00	1.50	.633
.65	.962	1.60	.612
.70	.926	1.70	.594
.75	.895	1.80	.577
.80	.867	1.90	.565
.85	.841	2.00	.547
.90	.817	2.10	.535

Index

120